BRAZIL

A·MASK·CALLED·PROGRESS

NEIL MacDONALD

AN·OXFAM·REPORT

British Library Cataloguing in Publication Data

MacDonald, Neil, *1950* -
Brazil : a mask called progress : an Oxfam report.
1. Brazil. Economic conditions
I. Title
330.981

ISBN 0-85598-091-5

Cover design incorporates a Kaxinawá painting of the sun.

Published by Oxfam, 274 Banbury Road, Oxford OX2 7DZ
Printed by Oxfam Print Unit

CONTENTS

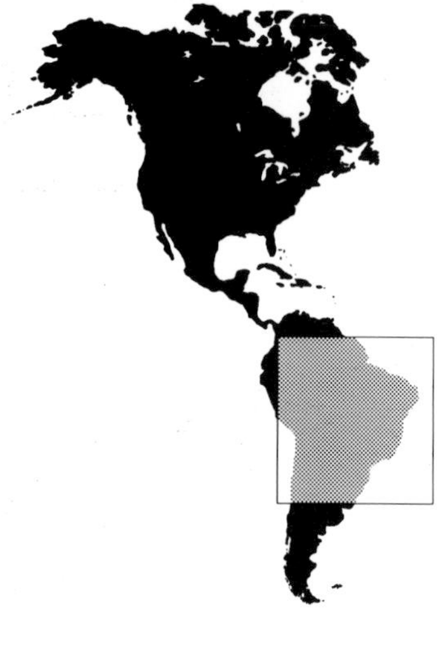

STATES:

1 ACRE
2 AMAZONAS
3 RORAIMA
4 PARA
5 AMAPA
6 MARANHAO
7 PIAUI
8 CEARA
9 RIO GRANDE DO NORTE
10 PARAIBA
11 PERNAMBUCO
12 ALAGOAS
13 SERGIPE
14 BAHIA
15 RONDONIA
16 MATO GROSSO
17 MATO GROSSO DO SUL
18 GOIAS
19 MINAS GERAIS
20 ESPIRITO SANTO
21 RIO DE JANEIRO
22 SAO PAULO
23 PARANA
24 SANTA CATARINA
25 RIO GRANDE DO SUL

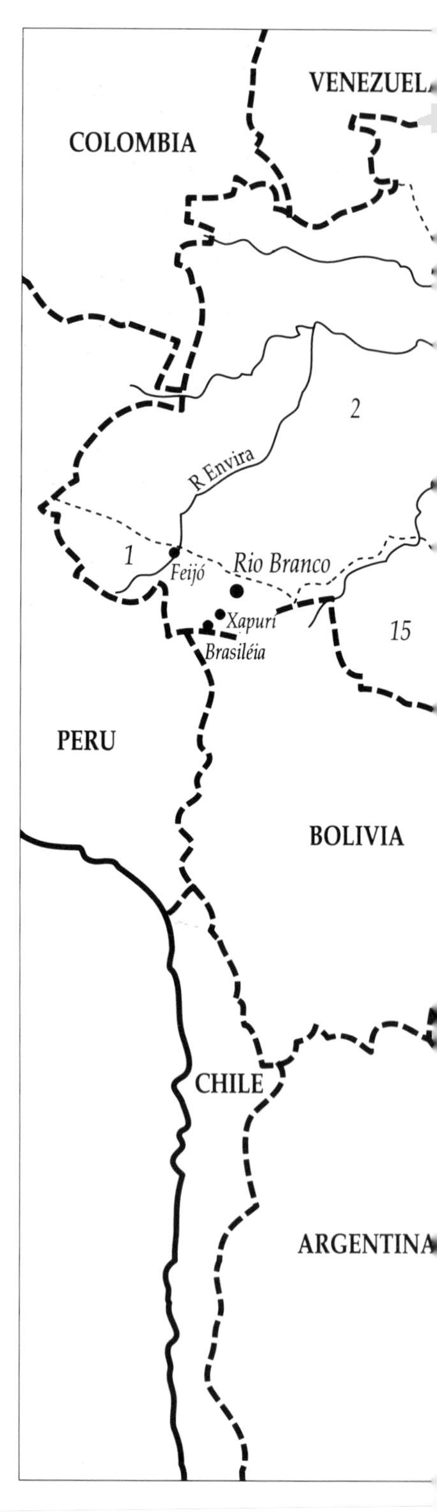

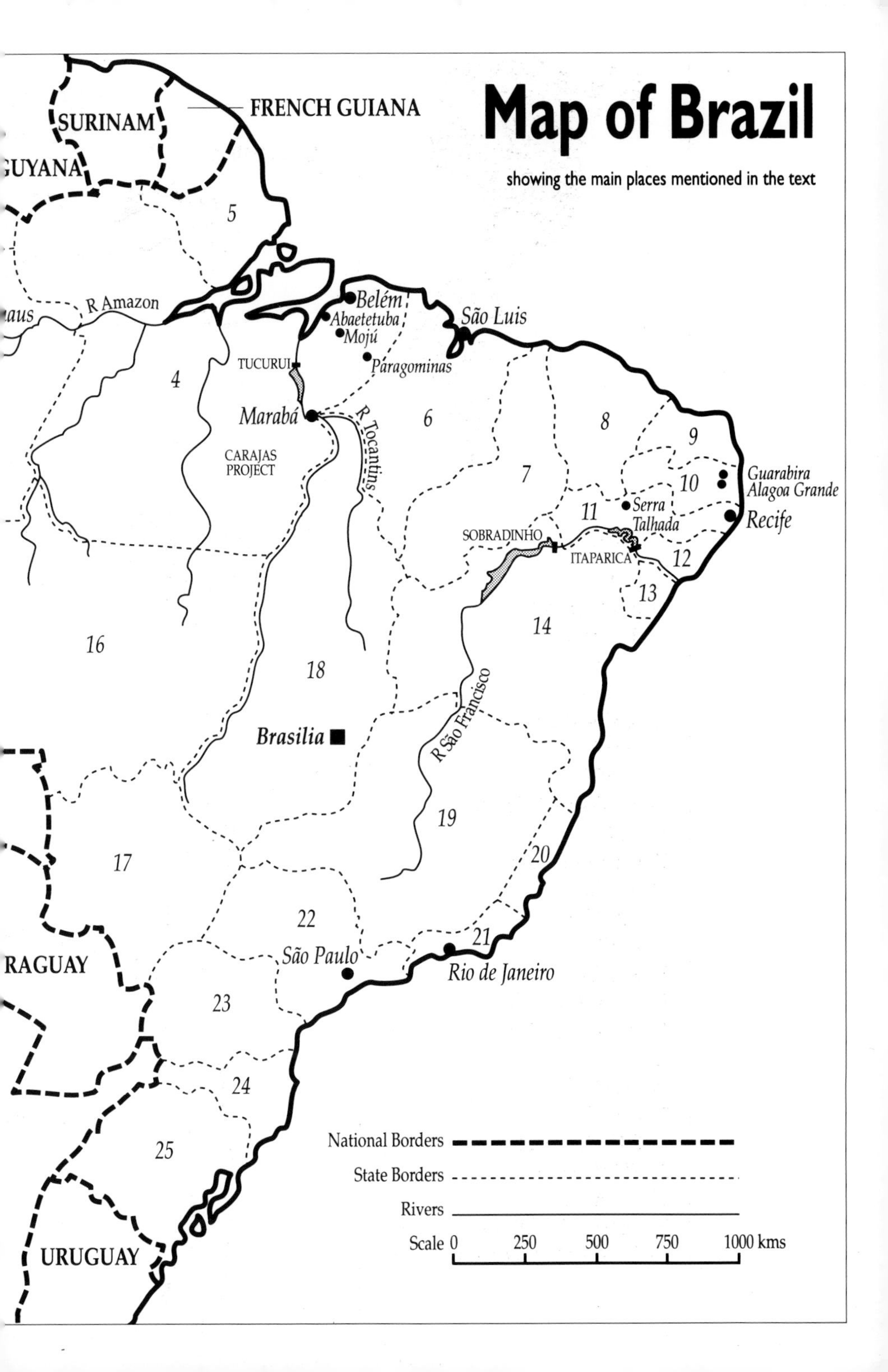

Map of Brazil
showing the main places mentioned in the text
FRENCH GUIANA
SURINAM
GUYANA
R Amazon
Belém
Abaetetuba
Mojú
Paragominas
São Luis
TUCURUI
Marabá
R Tocantins
CARAJAS PROJECT
Guarabira
Alagoa Grande
Serra Talhada
Recife
SOBRADINHO
ITAPARICA
R São Francisco
Brasilia
São Paulo
Rio de Janeiro
RAGUAY
URUGUAY
4
5
6
7
8
9
10
11
12
13
14
16
17
18
19
20
21
22
23
24
25
National Borders
State Borders
Rivers
Scale 0 250 500 750 1000 kms

BRAZIL: A MASK CALLED PROGRESS

INTRODUCTION

Construction of the Tucuruí dam, 1987.
(Julio Etchart)

"The edge of the world gets closer and closer every year."

Brazil is a country of immense contrasts: a Third World country with its own internal First World. The Tucuruí dam in the Amazon region could stand as a symbol of these contrasts.

The dam is a breath-taking sight. Its sheer sinuous length is impressive; the roaring water rolls through with such force that it appears to be solid; a cloud is continually regenerated from the water droplets thrown up by the dam, pinched off from the tail of spume, as if the entire structure was blowing smoke rings.

Tucuruí lies on the Tocantins river in the midst of the rainforest in the north of Brazil. With a generating capacity of 250 megawatts, it provides the power for the region all the way up to the city of Belém at the mouth of the Amazon, taking in the Albras aluminium refinery. This is the dam whose construction is featured in the film "The Emerald Forest", which concerns the confrontation between Brazil's own First and Third Worlds. In the film one of the Indian leaders says as the dam encroaches on their territory: *"The edge of the world gets closer and closer every year."*

The edge of Tucuruí's world is formed by a 20-mile fence, enclosing the dam and the new city that has grown up beside it. It makes all the difference in the world which side of the fence you live on. Tucuruí new town does not invite visitors. Its orbital road spirals for miles round the outside of the fence. You can see the neat, clean houses. But there's no way in. Finally you come to the security gate on the far side, guarded by armed police. This is the sole entrance to the city. Here are shopping malls, air-conditioning, movie theatres for the employees and functionaries of the dam. Outside are the mean shacks of the settlers and the now-neglected old town. These are the people the fence is meant to keep out.

Magnificent engineering feat it may be. But the human and environmental costs have been immense. The lake formed by the dam has flooded 243,000 hectares of forest, including much of the lands of the Waimiri-Atroari Indians —

Tucuruí dam. (John Magrath/ Oxfam)

of whom only 350 remain, compared with 6,000 at the turn of the century. A 100-yard-wide treeless swathe runs for hundreds of miles through the forest, carrying the electricity pylons from the dam. At some points this strip was cleared by spraying the forest with a defoliant which may be similar to the 'Agent Orange' used by US troops in Vietnam. As in Vietnam, there have been reports of birth defects from the population living in its path.

During the 1970s and 1980s other mega-projects besides Tucuruí were under construction: the huge dams at Sobradinho and Itaparica on the São Francisco river, the Alumar and Albras aluminium smelters, and the huge Greater Carajás ironfield with its 900-kilometre railroad. Giant projects for the development of a country the size of a continent: bigger than the whole of Europe, and 35 times the size of Britain. One economy is being uprooted and another planted. Brazil is going through the same process of social and economic transformation in a few decades that Britain went through in two centuries during the Industrial Revolution. The turmoil and the violence are correspondingly greater.

Whole communities have been uprooted by the construction of dams and factories; new roads bored into the Amazon rainforest are bringing waves of land-hungry settlers from the north-east and the south to the new 'frontier'. Settlers, forest dwellers and big ranching interests fight over the control of the frontier land. Small farmers, driven off their land, flood to the cities, to struggle for existence in miserable shanty towns.

Rich world, poor world

Brazil has riches in plenty. Until the Portuguese colonists came in 1500, it sustained 5 million Indians. Its gold, in the seventeenth and eighteenth centuries, flowed across the Atlantic to Portugal. This gold, which found its way to the London banking houses which held the Portuguese economy in debt, financed England's war against Napoleon. Its fertile coastal lands provided the 'white gold' of sugar for European tables in the sixteenth century. Today, coffee and soya are cultivated, as well as sugar; there are immense mineral deposits and industrial plants to process them, such as the giant car factories of São Paulo.

But Brazil is also a land of immense contrasts in wealth. In 1984, according to the Movement of Landless People, 4 per cent of the people owned 67 per cent of the cultivable land, while the poorest 71 per cent of people were squeezed on to 10.9 per cent of the land. These small farmers feed Brazil. Of the food staples, they provide almost 28 per cent of the rice, over 55 per cent of the maize, over 66 per cent of the beans, and almost 78 per cent of the manioc. But over two-thirds of them live below the poverty line, receiving only half the statutory minimum wage or less. Brazil is the world's second largest agricultural exporter, after the United States, yet malnutrition causes almost seven out of every ten deaths among children under five years of age.

Brazil is developing fast. At the end of the second world war, seven Brazilians in every ten lived in the countryside; today seven in every ten live and work in cities. Brazil is becoming an industrial power. But its development is leaving many people behind. Its gross domestic product makes it the eighth most powerful economy in the world; but two-thirds of the people live below the poverty line – the biggest disparity between rich and poor in the world. The jet-set

On the beach at Boa Viagem, Recife. (Jenny Matthews/ Oxfam)

beaches of Rio de Janeiro, with its world-famous carnival, coexist with the misery of the urban slums known as *favelas*.

The confrontation between rich and poor, between Brazil's own First and Third Worlds, has become a matter of international public concern in the last few years. The main focus has been on the destruction of the rainforest, over-exploitation of the environment and natural resources. How should the international community respond? Debt-environment swaps have been proposed in some circles. This means environmental groups or governments redeeming a part of Brazil's massive foreign debt (which amounts to US$112,000,000,000), in return for the Brazilian government agreeing to manage a part of the country in ways which are acceptable to these outside interests. This book challenges approaches which separate the problem of environment from the problem of development; and it rejects an approach which makes the debate one between Northern environmentalists, Southern governments and international lending organisations. It argues that the only approaches that will produce long-lasting solutions are those which are fully under the control of ordinary Brazilian people.

The book argues that the concern to protect the environment and the concern for a fair deal for Brazil's poor should be one and the same concern. It argues that any model of development which is unjust socially is also destructive environmentally; and that the best alternatives for protecting the environment are those being put forward by groups of poor people who are struggling to defend their livelihood and cultural existence within that environment. It argues that only approaches to development which sustain human beings will also sustain the environment.

This is not an abstract argument. It is based on over 20 years of Oxfam's work in Brazil, since an office was opened in 1969: indeed Oxfam has been supporting development efforts in Brazil since 1958. But the book is not primarily about Oxfam. It is about Brazilian people, their efforts and their work. There are no

On the streets in a slum area of Recife.
(C. Pearson/Oxfam)

Oxfam-run projects. Instead, Oxfam supports projects that are created and run by Brazilian people, our project partners. In 1989/90 Oxfam, from a local office in the north-eastern city of Recife, spent over one million pounds supporting these initiatives (a tiny fraction of the money invested by companies and loaned by international banks). Because of the current concern about the Amazon, much of the discussion in this book relates to the problems of that region. But the situation of the Amazon is also related to the problems of the impoverished and drought-afflicted north-east. Whether in the Amazon region or the north-east, this book is about how communities of poor people work together to create a few more choices, to gain a bit more control over their lives. It is an opportunity for them to tell their stories, and is written in the hope that people in the 'developed' world will join with them in their struggle for a secure future for themselves – which means a more secure future for us all.

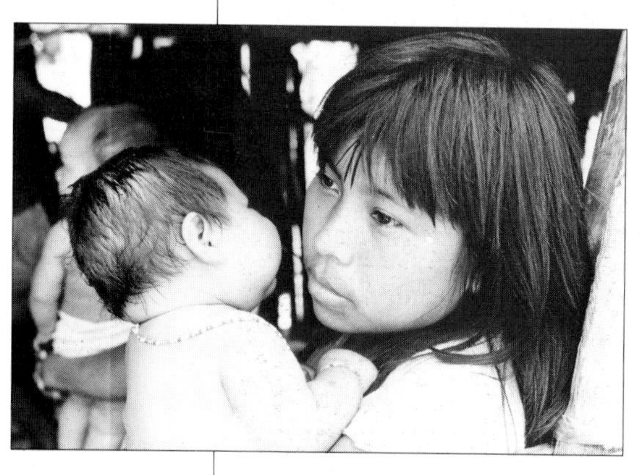

Kaxinawá Indians in the village of Paroá, Acre state.
(Jenny Matthews/Oxfam)

PART I: THE RAINFOREST PEOPLE

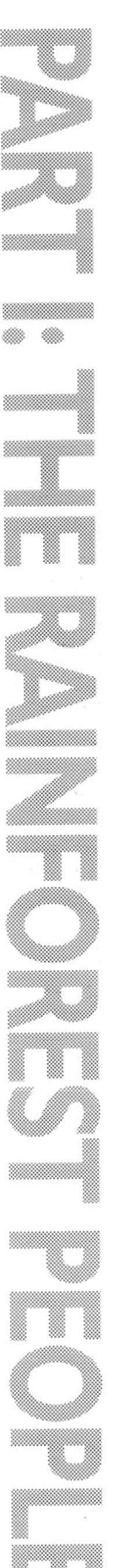

(Tony Gross/Oxfam)

Introduction

Seen from space, the only man-made structure visible on earth is the Great Wall of China. Opinions differ about what other visible evidence there is of human activity. North Americans claim that it is the lights of New York city. Brazilians, with a perverse pride, often say that it is the smoke from the burning of the Amazon rainforest. During the summer burning season, almost a quarter of a million fires are lit in the forest. Calculations suggest that around one acre of rainforest in every ten has already disappeared. And the rate of destruction is increasing: in 1975 just under seven million acres of land had been cleared; by 1980 four times as much had disappeared; and up to 1988 over 40 million acres had been cleared each year.[1] A Brazilian government survey published in 1990 revealed that in the 1988/89 season 11,366,400 acres (17,760 square miles) were destroyed – an area larger than Switzerland. Most of the cleared land is used for cattle ranching, a form of land speculation encouraged by government incentives. The logging industry, exploiting the valuable hardwoods of the forest, is the second major cause of deforestation. Mining and colonisation from the land-hungry south and north-east put added pressure on the forest.

The Amazon region contains about half of the world's remaining 5 million square miles of rainforest. It spans about 3 million square miles (almost the size of the continental United States), straddling Colombia, Peru, Ecuador, Bolivia, Venezuela, Guyana, Surinam, French Guiana and Brazil. Most of it is in Brazil. The rainforests in the equatorial belt of the world are part of the ecological maintenance system of the globe, and a treasure-house of resources. The forests regulate the world's climate. They clean the atmosphere, taking in carbon

Blazing forest on the route of a new road through Rondônia.
(Tony Gross/Oxfam)

dioxide, building the carbon into new growth, and releasing oxygen. As rainforests decrease, carbon dioxide, which traps heat, builds up, and so contributes to global warming through the greenhouse effect. Another climatic role of the rainforests is to absorb and slowly release moisture, regulating rainfall. Disturbing this balance can produce flood and drought. The Sahara Desert, a forested region in classical times, bears tragic witness to this. There is a growing concern in Brazil that deforestation may already be changing the climate. Rainfall in the drought-prone north-east has become sparser and more unpredictable in recent years.

The Amazon region is a reservoir of genetic diversity: of the five million or so different species on the planet, over one million are estimated to be in the Amazon. Destruction of the rainforest is destroying this genetic heritage, with potentially serious consequences for us all. Modern forms of intensive agriculture mean that more than 80 per cent of the world's food supply depends on fewer than two dozen species of plants and animals. Scientists and agricultural companies are beginning to look to the rainforests as a source of wild genes that can be bred back into these highly domesticated species, to sustain their ability to combat disease and adapt to new environments.

The world's rainforests also provide constituents for about a quarter of all our prescription drugs. Alkaloids from the leaves of the rosy periwinkle have been used to treat Hodgkin's disease and childhood leukaemia. The bark of the cinchona tree yields quinine, which is used in combatting malaria. A drug for treating high blood pressure was discovered in the venom of the Brazilian pit viper. Cures for cancer and for AIDS may lie in the Amazon too, but most species are disappearing faster than they can be catalogued. The alkaloid castanospermine, found in a species of alexa tree in the Amazon region and Madagascar, is being tested as a possible treatment for some forms of AIDS. Miguel Texeira Mendes, a rubber-tapper, lives deep in the forest in the western Amazon. He says, *"We don't need a health post. We've got more medicines here than a chemist's shop."*

The rainforest people like Miguel – the rubber-tappers, the Indians, the river people – are an inseparable part of the forest system. They are the practical conservationists, because their way of life depends on working in harmony with the forest. The forest yields them rubber and Brazil nuts as a source of cash income, and wild pigs and other animals as a source of meat. The rubber-tappers, like the Indians, clear small patches of the forest, which they farm for their basic needs of rice, beans, manioc and fruit for only three years at a time. The forest people manage this process of regeneration carefully. After the final harvest, they cut and burn what is left of the plants, and dig the ash, rich in nutrients, into the ground. Then they plant fast-growing forest species, which will take up the nutrients rapidly, and prevent them being washed away. In later seasons, the forest people encourage a longer-lived second generation of plants by weeding out some species, protecting others, fertilising and planting specially valuable trees, shrubs and fruits. They engineer the forest that is regenerated so as to provide fruits for themselves and food for the game they hunt. But it will be at least 30 years before they grow crops on the same patch again.

"We don't need a health post. We've got more medicines here than a chemist's shop."

The rainforest is a *managed* ecosystem, which has been transformed and preserved by the economic activity of the forest people. The Indians were the first to discover the medicinal uses of many of the plants from which the pharmaceutical companies now profit. Experiments by Indian farmers domesticated the forest's food plants and discovered the genetic and environmental conditions for successful cultivation. Today's new 'green' awareness has taught us about the interconnectedness of the global ecosystem. People like Miguel and the Indians remind us that human life is connected too to the fate of the planet – its destruction or its preservation. More and more people today are concerned about the fate of the Amazon rainforest. But the Amazonian ecosystem is not just trees; it is not a primeval forest which has existed unchanged since the birth of life on the planet. Protecting the rainforest and its resources does not mean keeping it free of people. The economic activity of the traditional forest people preserves and develops the forest. In contrast, the big ranching companies which have moved into the Amazon region exploit the forest in a different and destructive way. Protecting the rainforest means also supporting the forest people who are trying to defend their way of life.

Indians cultivating bananas, Acre state. (Jenny Matthews/ Oxfam)

"The forest is one big thing – it has people, animals and plants. There is no point in saving the animals if the forest is burned down. There is no point in saving the forest if the animals and people are driven away. Those trying to save the animals cannot win if the people trying to save the forest lose. The Indians cannot win if the others lose, and they won't be successful without the Indians' support – for we are the ones who know the forest. None of us is strong enough to win alone – together, we can be strong enough to win." (Paiakan, a Kayapó Indian)

THE RUBBER-TAPPERS: WORKING WITH THE FOREST

The rubber-tappers show clearly that people can develop the forest in ways that do not harm it. The first rubber-tappers were peasants from the other side of the country, the impoverished north-east. As the world market for rubber expanded, they were recruited as migrant male workers by the rubber estate managers. They have been in the forest since the end of the nineteenth century. The migrants intermarried with Indian women, from whom they learned how to work the forest. They milk the latex from the wild rubber trees and coagulate it into crude rubber. They take nothing from the forest that cannot be regenerated.

Fazendinha is a rubber-tapping community in the far north-west of Brazil near the border with Bolivia. Located in the forest near the town of Xapurí, the settlement is a collection of four houses and a schoolhouse. Fazendinha is a relatively well-off community: the people have a few cattle to supplement their agriculture and the collection of rubber and Brazil nuts. They collect rubber for eight months of the year, between May and December, and then collect Brazil nuts during the rainy season between January and April.

The forest is all around. Long shafts of sunlight lance at intervals through the canopy, creating little pools of brilliant light. Small mushrooms and the first shoots of young rubber trees poke through the detritus of mouldering leaves and sodden papery shells of dead trees. Yellow, black and red butterflies whirl like handfuls of confetti through the shafts of sunlight. Birds call high up in the canopy, near the tops of the forest giants.

Miguel Texeira Mendes lives in Fazendinha. He works three of the community's five *estradas*. An *estrada* is a trail linking around 150 rubber trees. Like most rubber-tappers, Miguel works each of his trails in rotation, leaving each to recover for three days after bleeding its trees for the raw latex. It is rare for women to tap rubber. Mostly, women's work is agricultural – sowing, weeding and harvesting the crops – on top of the domestic work which they perform alone. Miguel, like men everywhere, forgets his wife's economic contribution when he boasts: *"We produce up to 1,000 tins* [1 tin = 12 kilos] *of Brazil nuts here. I bring up five children. With 100 hectares,[2] without money from anyone to pay for anything, I can feed and clothe my family on my own. I'm my own boss. Rubber-tappers don't need to beg from anyone."*

The point, however is clear: knowing the forest, rubber-tapper communities are economically viable and largely self-sufficient. A rubber tree, properly milked, yields latex for 50 years or more. But the work is arduous. First a diagonal cut is made in the bark – not too deep, or the tree can become infected by mould and die. Then a metal channel is inserted into the bottom of the groove, for the latex to ooze out. The latex drips slowly into a container, often the halved gourd-like outer husk of a Brazil nut (*"We use everything"*, says Miguel). In the past, they would have to walk the trail twice a day, making the incisions in the morning and then coming back to collect the latex in the afternoon. This was important because if it rained, and water got into the raw latex, it would be spoiled. Then there was the laborious and choking process of smoking the latex to coagulate it. Nowadays everything is simpler, at least in the better-off communities: the tappers add an acid to the collecting cup which coagulates the latex directly, and allows it to be left for up to two days before collection.

Rubber-tapper at work near Xapurí, Acre.
(Wendy Tyndale/ Christian Aid)

When Miguel talks, it is clear how well he knows the forest:

> *"Trees are like people. Some are nice. Some are ugly. Some are so ugly we only look at them because we have to. This one looks as if it has warts. There are some people when you visit them who give you a coffee and kill a chicken for you. Then there are others who don't make you feel welcome at all. Trees are like that. There are some*

that give us pleasure by giving us a full cup of latex. Others just give us a little dribble. But we have to deal with them all."

Each tapper works alone, cutting his own trees on his own trails. But, as Miguel says, *"You can always call out and somebody will answer you"*. They sell their rubber jointly. But beyond that, each tapper goes his own way. All three families in the community together produce about 120 kilos of latex a month. The five communities in this area are trying to form a cooperative, *"to come together more"*, as Miguel puts it.

Coming together more is essential to a new range of survival skills that the rubber-tappers are having to learn. Because only together is their voice strong enough to resist a threat to their way of life that also threatens the very existence of the forest – the opening up of the Amazon region to the cattle companies.

THE RUBBER SOLDIERS

For a hundred years the rubber-tappers have been fighting poverty and degrading conditions. Their story is the story of rubber itself. Europeans first discovered rubber from the Amazon Indians in the eighteenth century. When Charles Goodyear stumbled on his 'vulcanisation' process for preserving rubber, he opened the way for a swelling market in the new water-proof substance. But it was not until the late nineteenth century, with the invention of the motor car and the demand for rubber tyres, that the rubber boom really began. Brazil had the best quality rubber trees, and, in the first decades of the twentieth century, the country supplied 70 per cent of the world's latex.

Suddenly the remote Amazon region became linked into the international trade system. The links ran from the rubber-tappers milking the latex to commodity traders in London and Paris, and factories in Europe and the United States. Great ocean-going liners plied a thousand miles up the Amazon to the river port of Manaus. Until the turn of the century Manaus had been a sleepy jungle town of a few thousand souls. By 1900 it had swelled to a population of 75,000. It was the capital of a glittering jungle society, boasting electricity, piped water, a tram service and an opera house that could seat 2,000 people. The pinnacle of this society was formed by the heads of the import-export houses, usually representing financial institutions in London or Paris. At the base of the society were the impoverished rubber-tappers, who lived as virtual serfs in remote forest estates they never left.

The rubber 'bosses' were the intermediaries. They recruited male migrant workers from the drought-prone north-east, where peasants thronged to the cities to find work. The bosses advanced them 'credit' for their journey across the country – locking them in a debt trap from which few ever escaped. Every kilo of latex they collected and coagulated just drove them deeper into debt, because their only source of supplies was the over-priced goods from the bosses' stores, again supplied on 'credit'.

Even before the rubber boom reached its height, it was already under threat. The British government wanted to break the Latin American monopoly of rubber,

"How can one man dominate all this as if he were God?"

and, in 1876, Henry Wickham smuggled 70,000 rubber seedlings down the Amazon and across the Atlantic to Kew Gardens. Experiments by Kew botanists finally succeeded in breeding hardy disease-resistant varieties. By the beginning of the first world war, Britain's Asian plantations in Ceylon and Malaya had overtaken Brazil's production. By the mid-1930s Amazonian rubber was only 1.4 per cent of a world production that had reached over one million tons.

The second world war brought a second boom to Brazilian rubber. The Japanese overran Britain's Asian rubber plantations, and the United States asked Brazil to revive Amazonian production. A 'Rubber War' was declared, and a new generation of 'rubber soldiers' was recruited, some 50,000 workers coming as before from the poverty-stricken north-east.

But, after the war, natural rubber again entered the doldrums. By the 1960s, many of the old landowners were selling up. For some rubber-tappers this meant a release from feudal bondage. For others, it was merely an exchange of exploitation by the landowner for exploitation by the middlemen. The middlemen carried on the tradition of debt-peonage by overcharging the tappers for the industrial goods they needed, such as ammunition and kerosene, and underpaying for the smoked latex.

Nevertheless, the 1970s gave the rubber-tappers a brief respite. Though some estate-owners survived, the old serfdom was ending. The modern ranching companies had not yet moved in. The tappers enjoyed a way of life that balanced the needs of humans and nature. The rubber was not very profitable, but their cash needs were few, and the forest supplied most of their needs. As a result, natural rubber production survived in the western Amazon. It employed about two-thirds of the population of the state of Acre, and provided about one-third of its income. But no sooner were the rubber-tappers beginning to live for themselves, than a new and more deadly challenge emerged – that of the new *fazendeiros* (ranchers) whose exploitation of the forest destroys it. For Miguel this is an incomprehensible way of behaving:

> *"Now we've bought the land. But now other people come and say it's theirs. I talked to this worker who was cutting down the forest and asked how much he was being paid by his boss. He said US$2 a day. I said, 'I can get $3 in 20 minutes from the rubber trees. And we're our own bosses.' These people want to dominate the world. How can one man dominate all this – 30,000 hectares and all the people in it – as if he were God?"*

As the old rubber-estate owners sold up, new ranching companies moved in, often bringing big money from the south, sweetened by government credits and tax breaks. The government of Acre in the western Amazon published adverts promoting investment which described the state as the 'fillet steak of the Amazon'. The rubber-tappers found themselves locked in an increasingly bitter fight for their forest.

The ownership of the forest is legally unclear. The rubber-tappers assert their rights to the land, as being at least as good as anyone else's. But often they are unaware that pieces of paper have been exchanged in the cities until a logging crew moves in and starts clearing the forest that feeds them.

LEARNING TO FIGHT FOR THE FOREST

With each tiny community of tappers isolated from the others, deep in the forest and far up rivers, often many days' journey from each other, it was difficult for them to meet, to discuss and to plan their response to the land grabs. And lack of education compounded the problem. In the late 1970s the rubber-tappers began to come up with solutions.

Schools in the forest: Project Rubber-Tapper

Education turned out to be the key to bringing the rubber-tappers together. A local voluntary group began *Projeto Seringueiro* (Project Rubber-Tapper), with initial funding from Oxfam and later funding from the local government. Project workers lived in the forest, working as rubber-tappers and winning the tappers' trust. Over time, they opened up the possibility of forming cooperatives so that the tappers could market their own rubber, and of establishing schools where they could learn to read and count so that the merchants couldn't cheat them.

Chico Mendes, the rubber-tappers' leader from Xapurí and child of rubber soldiers, described the importance of schooling.

> *"My life began just like that of all rubber-tappers, as a virtual slave bound to do the bidding of his master. I started work at nine years old, and, like my father before me, instead of learning my ABC, I learned how to extract latex from a rubber tree. From the last century until 1970, schools were forbidden on any rubber estate in the Amazon. The rubber-estate owners wouldn't allow it. First, because if a rubber-tapper's children went to school, they would learn to read and write and add up, and would discover to what extent they were being exploited. That wasn't in the bosses' interests. Also it was better for production to have the children available for work rather than going to school.*
>
> *So for many years, the great majority of us could neither read nor write. The rubber-tapper worked all year, hoping he would finally make a profit, but always remained in debt. As he couldn't count, he couldn't tell whether he was being cheated or not."*[3]

Despite suspicion from the ranchers, who told the security forces that the schools were a training camp for guerrillas, the tappers kept the project alive.

Agripino Pereira da Silva, 42-year-old father of six, is the teacher, or monitor as they are called, for the school at Fazendinha, in the north-west of the Amazon region. When the schools in the area started under the auspices of the rural workers' union in 1985, Agripino was chosen by the community as monitor: *"I haven't had any formal education. But I was always asking people to teach me things as a boy. Soon I was able to read and write."*

He had no difficulty passing the qualifying test for *Projeto Seringueiro* (which requires the equivalent of two years' schooling). He was given three months' training in 'what to teach and how to teach'. The project started simply as adult literacy and numeracy classes, but it has now been expanded to include children. When the school started, only five of the 50 people in the community were able to read and write. Now over 30 can. Even though students may have to walk up to an hour and a half to get to classes, the school is popular. There are 22 in the class, with places divided equally between adults and children and between men and women. Adults and children are taught together at the moment, but Agripino hopes that, with the help of his most able pupil, they will be able to divide into two classes – separating adults and children.

They teach using the 'Freire method'. Pioneered by Brazilian educationalist Paulo Freire, it puts learners and their knowledge, rather than teachers, at the centre of education. Agripino explained their method, starting with the textbook they use: *Poronga (Lamp)*:

> *"The idea is illuminating the path, making us see. So we can see how we were exploited by the bosses and the middlemen. We teach Portuguese in such a way that it's related to our life in the forest. We teach all about the animals, our food, unionisation, life in the city and how it's more difficult. We show how, when we live in the forest, we don't go hungry: we always have our game and our crops. People in the city who earn the minimum salary go hungry.*
>
> *Each lesson starts with a word:* mata *(forest), for example. We write it on the blackboard. We discuss it and what it means, our lives in the forest. The most interesting discussions are always about* mata *and* sindicato *(union). This is a good way to teach. I don't want them to swallow things without questioning."*

What, in Agripino's view, are the main benefits? *"People who couldn't count before can now do their sums and understand what's happening when they're trading. Besides that, it prepares people for struggles. It makes them more conscious of their rights and the need to organise."*

Rubber-tappers' literacy class near Xapurí, Acre. (Tony Gross/ Oxfam)

From education to action

The schools and cooperatives of *Projeto Seringueiro* had brought the rubber-tappers together. They took it from there: along with education has come organisation. The first rubber-tappers' unions were formed in 1975 in the town of Brasiléia and then in 1977 in the town of Xapurí. Others followed, and in 1985 the National Council of Rubber-Tappers was formed to coordinate their activities. Their organisations give them the power to defend their way of life and, with it, the forest. Their standard response to the deforestation that threatens their livelihoods and their environment has become the *empate* – a peaceful occupation of the threatened area. Chico Mendes described the technique:

> *"When we organise an* empate, *the main argument we use is that the law is being flouted by the landowners, and our* empate *is only trying to make sure the law is respected... When a community is threatened by deforestation, it gets in touch with other communities in the area. They all get together in a mass meeting in the middle of the forest and organise teams of people to take the lead in confronting the workers cutting down the trees with their chain-saws and so on – all this in a peaceful but organised way. These teams try and convince the workers employed by the landowners to leave the area. The rubber-tappers also dismantle the camps used by those workers to force them out. We are often attacked by the police, because the landowners always apply to the courts for police protection. ...*
>
> *At the same time as 100 or 200 colleagues are involved in the* empate, *standing in the way of the chain-saws and the scythes, we aim to have a team whose job it is to get information about what is happening back to Xapurí, where another group will make sure it travels all over Brazil and the rest of the world. This is something we have only recently started to organise.*
>
> *For us the important thing is to continue to make a political impact. We feel our resistance can produce results through pressure by the press and lobbying organisations, at both a national and international level. Our evaluation is that we should not go for a confrontation."*[4]

Chico Mendes was assassinated in December 1988 – an indication of the price that rubber-tappers' leaders have had to pay for defending their land. The assassination was met with international outrage, ironically strengthening the international support that was so central to Chico's strategy.

The rubber-tappers learned that the threats to their way of life come from far beyond the forest – from the company boardrooms in big cities, from the inter-governmental lending agencies like the World Bank and the Inter-American Development Bank, from the headquarters of transnational corporations. And they have developed a sophisticated set of responses. They have testified to the UN's Brundtland Commission on the environment and, with Oxfam's help, have lobbied the World Bank. They have built up an impressive range of alliances with Third World and Green movements in North America and Europe. But central to their efforts and their search for an alternative path of development is their own strength and their alliances in Brazil. They continue to strengthen their own local unions, on top of which they have built the National Council of Rubber-Tappers to help them speak clearly with one voice. And in 1989, together with Indian groups, they created the Alliance of Forest Peoples (whose manifesto is reproduced in Appendix 1 at the end of this book).

> *"To defend the Amazon you have to support the unions, the women's organisations, the residents' associations. Since Chico's death the press have started calling him an ecologist. But he always called himself a trade unionist. We don't see any distinction between environmentalism and trade unionism."*
> (Atanagildo 'Gatão' Matos, National Council of Rubber-Tappers)

The rubber-tappers' struggle for the forest goes on. To win it, they need international understanding of their concerns. They also need unity among the forest dwellers themselves, and this is not easily achieved. In many cases rubber-tappers have found themselves in competition with the Indians, whose claims on the land are equally pressing.

Gatão Matos, of the National Council of Rubber-Tappers, planting a tree in honour of Chico Mendes, Sheffield, England. (Chris James)

INDIANS: STRUGGLE FOR SURVIVAL

2

Indian groups in Amazonia have now joined with the rubber-tappers in the Alliance of Forest Peoples. Throughout Brazil, the Indians have been fighting for their land, their culture and their very survival for almost 500 years, since the first Portuguese arrived. Throughout the period of Portuguese rule, between 1500 and 1889, the Indian was seen simply as an animal – to be enslaved as a source of labour, or to be driven from valuable lands. The Indians resisted, and the colonial conquerors began to replace them by slaves imported from Africa. After this, genocide became the most frequent Indian policy of the Portuguese. The *bandeirantes*, Portuguese adventurers, pressing into the forest in search of gold and silver, massacred them by the thousands. The seventeenth-century explorer Pedro Teixeira boasted that after 30 years of expeditions along the Negro and Amazon rivers, he had been responsible for the deaths of two million Indians. The Indians fought back, but with tragic losses.

In 1500 there were estimated to have been five million Indians in Brazil. Today there are only around 213,000. Most live in Amazonia, though Indian communities survive in the north-east and the south as well. They are divided into 150 different peoples, speaking 100 different languages.

Integration of the Indians, rather than massacre, has been the dominant theme of government policy during the twentieth century. But the results have often been equally deadly for populations suddenly plunged into the poverty, sickness and death that accompany contact with the dominant culture.

A NEW THREAT

With the opening of the Amazonian frontier, Indian lands have become valuable property. In 1982, at a Congress on the occupation of the Amazon, Jorge Teixeira, governor of Rondônia, said that it was 'absurd' that Indians should occupy 200,000 hectares of land in his state; he felt that they were an obstacle to progress, and that five hectares a piece would be enough for them. This estimate assumes that the Indians use land solely for intensive agriculture. In practice, the large areas they traditionally inhabit are important not only for the cultural and religious significance of certain sites, but also for ecologically sustainable use of the forest: the Indians collect forest products over a wide area and use fields for only a short time, to avoid exhausting the fragile soil.

Speaking of the onslaught on Indian lands, Ailton Krenak, the President of the Union of Indian Nations (UNI), has warned:

> *"The great mountains, until yesterday guardians of the last refuge of this people, are being shaken by violence, the son of greed. The rivers and streams, our younger brothers, are dredged and fatally wounded. The animals disappear in the voraciousness of the adventurers who seek instant riches. The last sacred regions of the Yanomami universe are threatened.*
>
> *The day will come when the great prophecy of the sons of Omam* [the Original Being, according to Yanomami religion] *will be fulfilled: 'When the sacred places are touched, the night will come, it will come like the morning breeze, for I shall be weakening. The night will come like the wind, for I shall be dying.'"*

To avoid this fate, the Indians have begun to organise themselves to defend their interests. The UNI is one result. The Indians also have the support of progressive white groups, such as the Catholic Church's missionary organisation (CIMI), the secular Pro-Indian Commission (CPI), and the Ecumenical Centre for Documentation and Information (CEDI).

FIGHTING FOR LAND AND MAKING IT WORK

Demarcation is the principal demand of many Indian nations. They want the State to recognise the land belonging to the Indians, and to defend their right to control that land. Under Brazilian law, all Indian lands were supposed to have been recognised and mapped out by 1978, but two-thirds of all Indian lands have still to be officially demarcated. There have, however, been successes, as the case of the Kaxinawá Indians illustrates.

Getting the land

The River Envira in the westernmost part of the state of Acre runs muddily down from the Peruvian border. Here the first demarcation of Indian lands in the state of Acre took place on what used to be rubber estates. The struggle to gain control of their lands united Indians who had previously been divided by traditional enmity, suspicion and competition. Divisions continue to exist, but they have discovered that solving their main problems needs all of them to act together.

Oxfam has been supporting the Kaxinawá and the other Indians of the Envira to gain more control over their lives. The Kaxinawá live in the western part of Acre, on the Envira and Jordão rivers. Originally they had lived as farmers in what is now Peru, until the rubber boom at the turn of the last century expelled them brutally. When the last great chief of the Kaxinawá died, the community scattered, falling prey to estate bosses on the look-out for cheap labour. The chief's son, Chico, tells how he became one of the labourers:

"I worked for three years on the estate. Then I moved to the frontier and worked on clearing the forest for cattle. The boss was called Barraso. I remember how he would come and stand with his hands on his hips and a cigarette in his mouth while the Indians worked at his feet. When there were whites here, in the time of the boss, our children didn't have education, didn't have medicine. Under the boss we had to beg for sugar and for salt in order to live. Now things are better."

Portrait of a chief

Chico Barbosa is the chief of the Kaxinawá village of Paroá. His shirt is faded and torn. His feet are caked with the mud of the river bank. But his bearing is proud. He is responsible for a community of 336 people, a handful on the river bank and the majority living deep in the forest as rubber-tappers. An Indian chief does not rule in the way that a white leader does. His status comes not from what he acquires, but from what he gives. His power is not the power of command, but of persuasion and of correctly interpreting the will of the community. He says, *"If I told people to do something they didn't want to do, they'd choose another chief."* He carries a heavy burden and has already tried to give it up once. He must worry all the time about the community's affairs, about defending its land, about resolving family squabbles. Long after the Amazon night has fallen and the sound of outboard motors on the river echoing off the banks and the clouds has been replaced by the night cries from the forest, the oil lamp burns in Chico's front room. His palm-thatched wooden house is not only home to his family of seven, but also acts as a drop-in centre for the community. They come to share his water and food, to listen to the football on the radio, or just to chat. He is tired of the responsibility. Though his father and his father before him were chiefs, Chico has given the community until 1994 to find a replacement.

Chico Barbosa
(Jenny Matthews/ Oxfam)

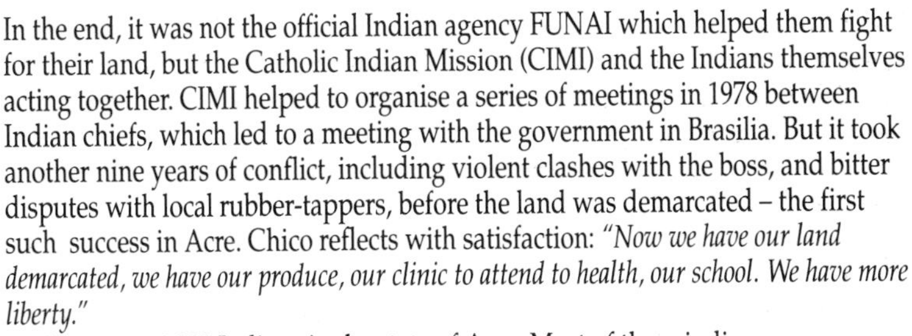

In the end, it was not the official Indian agency FUNAI which helped them fight for their land, but the Catholic Indian Mission (CIMI) and the Indians themselves acting together. CIMI helped to organise a series of meetings in 1978 between Indian chiefs, which led to a meeting with the government in Brasilia. But it took another nine years of conflict, including violent clashes with the boss, and bitter disputes with local rubber-tappers, before the land was demarcated – the first such success in Acre. Chico reflects with satisfaction: *"Now we have our land demarcated, we have our produce, our clinic to attend to health, our school. We have more liberty."*

There are 14,000 Indians in the state of Acre. Most of these indigenous communities have now resolved their land questions peacefully, by negotiation, with non-Indians such as rubber-tappers on their territory.

Working the land

Mapping out their land and getting official recognition for it is just the first step. Now they must make their land work so they can hang on to it. The Kaxinawá of Paroá produce rubber from the trails of the old estate. Agriculture too plays a big part in their economy. In temporary clearings in the forest, the Indians grow manioc, rice, beans, maize, peanuts, sweet potatoes and a variety of fruits, including oranges, tangerines, coconuts, graviola and mangoes. Men and women share agricultural tasks, with men doing the heavy work of deforesting and

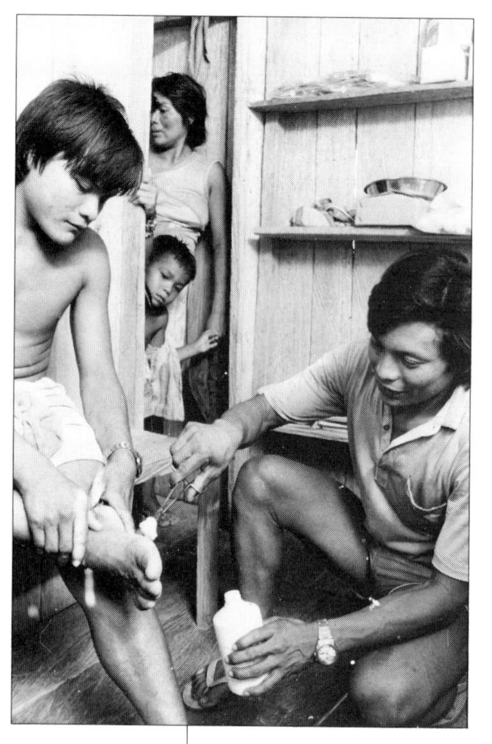

Rubens Barbosa, the village health monitor, at work in the community clinic, Paroá village. (Jenny Matthews/ Oxfam)

clearing the ground, and both sexes planting, weeding and harvesting.

But for the Kaxinawá, life is still hard. A century of contact with white society means that they are very much part of the cash economy. Their needs include a lot of goods they cannot produce themselves. They have to depend on the town of Feijó, two hours up-river, for salt, soap, kerosene, clothes, sugar, milk, butter, bread and coffee and meat to supplement their own coffee crop and the meat they get from hunting. But the marketplace does not favour them. The town shopkeepers, many of whom are the resentful former owners of rubber estates, charge them high prices. And the prices they get for their own produce are low. Adding the costs of transport, it can be hard to make ends meet. They have to market about a third of all the maize and rice they produce and anything up to half their bananas.

Chico's son Rubens is the powerhouse behind two of the community's attempts to respond. Two doors down from Chico's house on the river bank is the small cooperative managed by Rubens. It stores and sells the rubber that the Kaxinawá rubber-tappers bring in from the deep forest. The cooperative also helps to keep down the price of their purchases by buying in bulk. Four houses further on is Rubens' other responsibility – the clinic. He has a limited training as a health monitor (paramedic). He sees around 50 patients a month, who suffer from ailments like fever, diarrhoea, flu and skin diseases. A doctor from the state capital, Rio Branco, visits occasionally. Most of the medicine is industrial, though they are trying to regain the knowledge of plant remedies that the older people used to have. Women too retain some of the old knowledge. Since they are responsible for all the household tasks except the collection of firewood, they bear the first responsibility for their families' health.

Between the clinic and the cooperative is the school. The community have their own Kaxinawá teacher and an enrolment of 43 students. Education, however, is a double-edged weapon. All the teaching is in Portuguese: Kaxinawá is taught as a special subject. The Kaxinawá recognise the danger of their culture becoming swamped by that of the whites.

Slowly, the Kaxinawá have begun to improve the quality of their lives, and with it their control over their future. A small grant from FUNAI allowed them to buy five head of cattle, which have now multiplied to 35. They pay two white men to help them care for the cattle. They are both called Raimundo, and the Kaxinawá distinguish between them by calling them 'Clean Raimundo' and 'Dirty Raimundo'. Another small grant helped them buy tools to work the rubber. They have some funding to help them improve the cooperative. They bought a boat, with a grant from Oxfam. It shuttles up and down the river between Paroá and the town, keeping people in touch with each other, and making it easier to take their goods to market. But the projects the Kaxinawá want supported are always small ones. Chico explained why: *"We never make big projects; always small, to help a little. But we don't want to become dependent on projects. So long as we have our plantations and our animals, we live simply, but we get by."*

Working for unity on the river – OPIRE

This philosophy also lies behind the support that Oxfam has given. Big money can create dependency, rather than solving problems. The boat is intended not just for marketing but to bring Indians together so they can find their own solutions. In November 1988 the Indians of the river came together to form OPIRE – the Organisation of the Indian Peoples of the River Envira. OPIRE has a small headquarters in Feijó, as well as a house where Indians doing their marketing can stay. Oxfam has provided a motor boat for OPIRE to help improve communications.

OPIRE also runs a hospital to which Indians from the length of the river can come for treatment. The Catholic Indian Mission (CIMI) provides financial support and the Union of Indian Nations (UNI) provides a doctor.

OPIRE still has to deal with internal divisions. A history of mutual hostility and suspicion takes time to overcome. The Kaxinawás' neighbours, the Kulinas, once feared them as cannibals. The proud hard-working Kampas from the head of the river call themselves the 'true people' and are contemptuous of the others. The Katukina, who live just the other side of the river from the small town of Feijó, pride themselves on being civilised and knowledgeable in the ways of the town. Often they have acted as middlemen, trading the produce of the other Indians and cheating them in the process. The Katukina and the Kaxinawá tend to control OPIRE because they live closest to the town.

There is also a difference between the younger more educated people, from whom OPIRE's officers are drawn, and the older chiefs like Chico. While the older chiefs are most concerned about their own communities' problems, Julio, Chico's nephew and the coordinator of OPIRE, insists that OPIRE can only deal with general issues and that the communities must deal with their own problems.

Oxfam-funded boat on the River Envira, Acre state, taking people and goods to market in Feijó. (Jenny Matthews/ Oxfam)

This difference of opinion about OPIRE's role is not simply between young and the old or even between the general and the particular. It represents the gap between two cultures. Traditionally, Indian meetings must begin with a clearing of the air – a resolution of any family disputes or quarrels – in order that the business of the meeting can be conducted in harmony. The young are trying to avoid this and work in a way more like that of the white society. OPIRE is still far from having solved the problems of the Envira River Indians. But it gives them a clearer voice in determining their future.

YANOMAMI – TIME RUNNING OUT

Not all Indian groups have been as successful as the Kaxinawá in getting their land rights recognised. The Yanomami have been campaigning for the demarcation of their lands as a Yanomami park. They have suffered the cruel fate of seeing their land recognised and then losing part of it. Today, demarcation has become literally a matter of life and death for the Yanomami as they try to survive the invasion of their territory by gold prospectors.

The Yanomami are the largest Indian nation in Brazil, and the largest indigenous group in Latin America still living according to their original traditions. They live in extended family groups in communal houses known as Yano or Xabono. They cultivate manioc, tobacco, sweet potatoes and other tubers. Each extended family has its own plot of land. They are also hunters, fishers and gatherers. The women fish, gather fruit and wood for the cooking, cook and look after the children. The men hunt and sometimes gather fruit. Both sexes share agricultural work – the men preparing the ground and planting, while the women tend the plantations and harvest the crop. Their territory spans the border between Brazil and Venezuela. Of some 20,000 Yanomami, just under half live in Brazil.

Though the imperial Portuguese government knew of the Yanomami as early as 1707, the first substantial contacts with white culture occurred only in 1950. In the 1970s, the onslaught on Yanomami land began, as elsewhere in Brazil, with the construction of a highway, as part of the military government's programme to open up Amazonia. New settlers brought influenza, measles, tuberculosis, venereal diseases and other illness, to which the Indian communities had no resistance. They died in their hundreds. But the final offensive came when gold was discovered in Yanomami land in 1987 and 100,000 poor men flooded in, desperately seeking to strike it rich. By the beginning of 1990 there were still 40,000 gold panners in Yanomami territory. Davi Yanomami, a leader of his people, describes the death the gold prospectors brought in their wake – death by pollution, by disease, by murder.

Davi Yanomami
(Robert Davis/ Oxfam)

> *"They are destroying the rivers with the mercury* [used to separate gold from its ore], *the oil from the machines and the mud. The fish that the people eat, the water that they drink, makes them sick.*
>
> *The gold prospectors leave the land full of holes. Water collects in them and*

stagnates. This forms a breeding ground for the mosquitos. The prospectors brought malaria. It's spreading all over the territory. For example, in the Xidea region there are many landing strips. From there they fan out on foot, creating a network as they spread over the hills and valleys. [The regions of] *Parafure, Parahore, Maita, Xamatare – these places are all contaminated: everyone is sick with malaria, with flu, pneumonia, skin diseases.*

The gold prospectors use the Yanomami for target practice – they shoot us for no reason, just for fun. The Yanomami are revolted that women and children are being killed. They have revolvers, rifles, machine-guns, dynamite. We just have spears and bows and arrows."

"The gold prospectors shoot us for no reason, just for fun."

The gold prospectors have also begun to inflict deep changes on Yanomami society, as Davi Yanomami explains:

"At first they tried to make friends with the Yanomami. They promised a lot of things – food, rice, farinha [manioc flour], *tinned meat, sardines, old clothes, cooking pots. Then the Yanomami saw that they were being tricked. They say the Yanomami are lazy, that they do nothing – only sleep – that they live from begging. But the truth is that the prospectors have made it so that there is only the food that they bring – they have made it that way. There is no more food now, no more game, no more fish. They have been driven away by the pollution and the prospectors. So they make the Yanomami work for them as slaves – just so they can get a plate of food. They also use the Yanomami women – that's the way they get sick until they die. In Mucajai there is venereal disease and alcoholism. They make the people drink and then they get used to alcohol and then they get sick."*

Oxfam has been supporting the health team and other teams of the CCPY (Commission for the Creation of the Yanomami Park) since it was formed in 1979. In 1984 the government agreed to recognise a 7-million hectare Yanomami Indigenous Park. But it was never demarcated. In 1989 new government decrees created two national forests and a national park on the Yanomami land; this left the Yanomami with only 30 per cent of their land, scattered among 19 separate islands of territory.

Until 1989 the Brazilian government turned a blind eye to the hundreds of illegal landing strips and the activities of the prospectors. Only a change in government policy could save the Yanomami. Within Brazil and internationally, support began to grow. The powerful Kayapó Indians announced in 1989 that they were rallying to the side of the Yanomami. Davi Yanomami's work as a voice of his people was recognised when he was awarded the UN's 'Global 500' prize for defence of the environment (the year after Chico Mendes won it). However, he is thinking of returning the prize because he sees white people continuing to destroy Yanomami land. He made a powerful plea for action to end the pitting of poor whites against powerless Indians in an open letter he wrote to 'all the people on earth' in August 1989:

"The gold diggers and the illegal settlers don't have land: if they did, they wouldn't invade ours. I also see the white men suffering in the cities because they don't have a

"The rivers, the fishes and the forests are asking for help, but the government does not hear them."

place to live, they don't have food. Everybody has been suffering. They worry about this all, but they don't have courage to pressure the President. He is also deceiving his own people because he has been ordered by other countries to destroy our land, to build roads and to extract minerals. The government has also been instructed by other rich men when he borrows some money from abroad and uses it to ill-treat our land. The rivers, the fishes and the forests are asking for help, but the government does not hear them.

The government says we would die of starvation if the gold digging areas were closed down. But if they aren't closed down, for sure we will die of starvation. If they stop the gold diggers, we will plant plantains, banana, cocoyams, pawpaws, sugar cane, pejibaye palms, and so nobody is going to die. We Yanomami want to have our own land. We don't want our culture destroyed. So far we haven't lost our language, or our culture; that's why we are still fighting. This government is [meant to be] our leader but it has not been running the country properly in order to give peace and a good life to the Brazilian people."

In October 1989 in the face of growing pressure, a High Court ruling ordered the prospectors removed from Yanomami land. The Federal Police were ordered to begin the removal in January 1990. At the same time, an emergency health programme was to be implemented. However, the governor of Roraima, under pressure from the prospectors, signed a new accord. This allowed the prospectors to leave voluntarily instead of being removed forcibly. The accord was agreed by outgoing President Sarney. The prospectors then began to move out of the gold areas within the Yanomami islands and into one of the National Forests on the larger disputed Yanomami territory.

A bizarre legal battle then ensued, which was described by a federal prosecutor as throwing into question the institutions of Brazilian society. The High Court accused the government of violating the October court order; this order, the judges argued, applied to the entire 94 million hectare Yanomami territory, and not just the 'islands', and meant that government action in these areas was illegal until the case was resolved. The Executive backed down and agreed to removal of the prospectors from all disputed territory within 90 days, leaving the problem to be resolved by the incoming government of President Collor. Public concern grew internationally. In the UK, the Prince of Wales made a highly publicised statement of concern, and, after briefings from Oxfam and other agencies, Sir James Spicer introduced an Early Day Motion in the House of Commons calling for urgent action, which was signed by 138 MPs.

Collor visited the region in April 1990, and threatened to bomb the airstrips on which the prospectors depended for supplies. Some illegal airstrips were bombed by the government's 'Operation Yanomami' in succeeding months. But prospectors remained, and reopened airstrips almost as fast as they were destroyed. Many who had left the area during the rainy season returned later, despite a renewed warning by the High Court that this was illegal under the October 1989 ruling. 'Operation Yanomami' was extended beyond its December 1990 cut-off date. By the end of 1990, attempts to demarcate the full Yanomami territory, though supported by FUNAI, had reached stalemate.

THE LEGAL POSITION OF INDIANS

In May 1988, as members of the Brazilian Congress filed into the Parliament to debate the Indian clauses of a new constitution, they were greeted by Kayapó and other Indian warriors with painted faces and carrying spears. Modern parliamentary lobbying techniques had joined the Indians' arsenal of weapons.

Kayapó Indians lobbying Congress in Brasilia, April 1988: campaigning for Indian rights to be enshrined in the new Constitution. (John Magrath/ Oxfam)

The Indians remained in Brasilia, Brazil's purpose-built futuristic capital, throughout the debate. Their lobbying paid off. The new constitution recognises Indians as adult citizens of Brazil with the right to vote, and guarantees their possession of the land they inhabit, together with their surface resources. But between paper and reality there is an enormous gulf. Political will, as well as appropriate laws and resources, is needed to bridge this gulf.

Under the old military constitution Indians were regarded as legal minors, wards of the state Indian agency FUNAI. FUNAI in turn was simply the agency responsible for executing the policy drawn up by the military government. FUNAI drew up an Indian Statute, which became law in 1973, that recognised the Indians' right to remain on their lands and to own any wealth derived from them. But the loopholes in the Statute were telling: the government was authorised to intervene in Indian lands 'in the interests of national security', 'in order to carry out public works in the interests of national development', and 'to explore the riches of the subsoil if they are of outstanding interest for national security and development'.

General Jeronimo Bandeira de Mello, who was president of FUNAI between 1970 and 1974, stated that he did not believe that the Indians should be allowed to hold back the progress of Brazil, and that his main goal was to integrate the Indians into the modern nation state. Though subsequent heads of FUNAI were more moderate in their outlook, they did not fundamentally disagree. Many

Indians and their supporters are deeply sceptical about FUNAI's record in protecting Indian rights. One pro-Indian worker put it this way: *"FUNAI's role is supposed to be to protect Indians, but it protects them only in order to gain time to 'tame' them so that it will be easier for the companies to enter."*

The Indians increasingly want respect for their own culture and way of life. But the community-based decision-making that characterises Indian government, and the shared use of the land that typifies their economy, have not sat well with officialdom. The government today remains at odds with the diverse cultures of the Indians. Concerned to build the unity of the Brazilian nation, the government sees the existence of separate Indian nations as an anachronism. Official policy interprets unity to mean uniformity, ruling out a concept of Brazil as a multi-ethnic society (despite its Portuguese, Indian and African roots). As such, UNI, the Union of Indian Nations, is not officially recognised.

A major threat to the new constitutional rights is a 'catch-22' which removes the rights of what are called 'acculturated Indians'. This group of Indians are said to have integrated into white society, and are to inhabit 'colonies' instead of having the right to have their land demarcated. The concept of 'acculturated Indians' appears nowhere on the statute books: the law distinguishes only between Indians and non-Indians. Yet, as an internal statute used by FUNAI, the concept of 'acculturation' continues to determine practice, especially in areas that the military designates as important for national security, such as frontier zones.

A worker for a pro-Indian organisation described the colonies as being for 'Indians without culture'. The colonies do not correspond to the traditional territory of a given Indian nation. Indians of different nations may be lumped together within these areas. And the economic activity (agriculture, fishing, and mining) within the colonies corresponds not to the traditional way of life of the Indian communities, but to government decisions about how to use the land.

Who then are these 'acculturated' Indians? FUNAI says that if a non-Indian object is found within an Indian community, the community is 'in the process of acculturation'; equally so if it trades its surplus with a non-Indian community. So the discovery of even a matchbox would in the extreme case be theoretically sufficient for a community to lose its claim to respect for its traditional rights, land and customs. As one Indian leader, Zé Correia of the Jeminaua, says: *"If Indians are tough and resist, they are called animals. If they are 'civilised', they aren't called Indians. Hence there are no Indians!"*

But in many areas less sensitive than the militarised frontiers, the FUNAI definitions are being dropped. Instead, definitions which correspond to the Indians' own cultural practices are being used. Among the Kaxinawá community at Paroá on the Envira River, for example, are Indians with red or blond hair. They wear jeans and T-shirts, and travel in canoes powered by outboard motors. What defines any of them as Kaxinawá is not their hair colour or blood type (criteria which FUNAI used in the past) or their economic activity, but rather their acceptance by the community as Kaxinawá. There is growing recognition that there is no such thing as a pure and static culture among Indians, any more than there is among whites. Indian cultures evolve, assimilating influences from outside, without losing their own identity.

On the River Envira, Acre. (Jenny Matthews/ Oxfam)

THE GROWING INDIAN VOICE

In the 1970s a pro-Indian lobby and an independent Indian voice began to emerge. An important event in paving the way for this was the change in the Brazilian Catholic Church, under the influence of the new Latin American 'theology of liberation'. This led the Church to reorganise its own Indian missionary arm – CIMI – which became part of the pro-Indian lobby, working to assist the Indians' own initiatives.

A series of assemblies, starting in 1974, began to bring together some of the Indian leaders to discuss common problems. By 1980 Indian leaders who had attended these meetings proposed the formation of a Union of Indian Nations (UNI). FUNAI and the military government objected, but 73 leaders from 32 tribes founded UNI at a meeting in São Paulo in May 1981. Other groupings of Indians began to emerge too at regional levels, some, like the Envira River Indians' organisation OPIRE, linked to UNI, and others independent of it.

The power of the new Indian lobby became clear in July 1983, when Colonel Leal was replaced as head of FUNAI by a civilian. This followed the protest occupation of the FUNAI building by 14 Xavante Indians. The Indian nations had begun to outgrow the paternalistic care of FUNAI, and even the liberal patronage of the Church. They were doing things for themselves. They had learned that if they united they could challenge the power of white society.

Anselmo Fornerk, coordinator in Acre state of the Catholic church's CIMI, thinks time is running out. CIMI, with funds from Oxfam, assists in the areas of health training, education, economic activity and legal aid. CIMI-Acre works

"Once they've finished the road from Porto Velho, this area's going to explode with migration."

with ten main Indian groups in Acre itself, plus another two in southern Amazonas. The neighbouring state of Rondônia is currently a magnet for colonisation. Anselmo sees its experience as a warning sign for Acre:

> *"One third of the Indians of Rondônia were finished off culturally by the construction of the main road there, with funds from the Inter-American Development Bank. The tendency is for each group to be limited to its own little world and not know what's going on around it. You've either got to help them to resist or you can't expect them to do anything except lament when the disaster happens. It's not just us. We encourage the Indians to travel. UNI has been visiting the areas. That has had a lot of impact. But they don't have funds for this, so we help them out. We realise how important this is at the moment. Once they've finished the road from Porto Velho* [Rondônia] *this area's going to explode with migration. The timber industries are already arriving in the area."*

But Anselmo does not feel hopeless. He believes the Indians have a chance:

> *"When you see groups becoming organised and improving their economy, it gives you hope.* [It seems like] *we expect miracles, but if you look back over the last ten years at how the movement has grown, you couldn't have expected them to have done better. They were scattered in little communities like rubber-tappers. Communities which ten years ago had 30 people now have 300. They have grown not only in size, but also in strength. They are resisting and protecting their areas."*

The Indians, like the rubber-tappers, are finding and stating clearly that they are the best guardians of their own interests. And, in fighting together for their voice to be heard, they are at the same time fighting for a different vision of what development can mean.

(Jenny Matthews/Oxfam)

Introduction

The conflict over different forms of development in the Amazon region stems from broader conflict elsewhere in Brazil. The way in which land is used is at the heart of this conflict. Big farms in the south and the north-east producing sugar, coffee, soya and beef for export have gradually pushed subsistence farmers out of the most fertile regions. The small farmers have been driven to the very edge of survival in the harsh arid interior of the country. As land has become scarcer, more and more poor farmers have been violently evicted from their lands by the big farmers' hired gunmen. The small farmers demanded government action to guarantee them land. In the north-east, for example, a strong and growing movement of the rural poor, the *Ligas Camponesas*, asked for a land reform that would transfer ownership of under-used land to them. This created an explosive political situation.

In the 1960s, the military government that ran Brazil between 1964 and 1985 looked to the Amazonian frontier as a safety valve – a way of releasing pressure on the land without challenging the vested interests of the rich. The government promised a 'land without people for people without land'. Of course, the Amazon was already populated – by Indians, rubber-tappers and river-dwellers, described in the previous chapters.

But even for the new colonists, the promised land proved to be a mirage. The weak soils were not suited to their agricultural methods. Despite this, land values began to skyrocket, and big investors followed the small colonists into the Amazon. The old conflict over land had simply been exported to the Amazon.

Land conflicts

Land conflict is usually conflict between big proprietors and small farmers or landless rural people. According to the Brazilian Institute for Social Action and Education (IBASE), 12 million rural people have no land, or not enough land to survive on. At the same time, IBASE estimates that 2.8 million square kilometres of land are lying idle. Four and a half million people own land, but the majority of it is in the hands of 170,000 people. The 18 biggest landowners in Brazil together own a staggering 180,000 square kilometres – bigger than the Republic of Ireland, Holland and Switzerland put together. The biggest of the big 18 is the Manasa company, which owns over 41,000 square miles – about the size of Holland. Under these circumstances, land conflicts in Brazil have become increasingly violent. The Catholic Church's Pastoral Land Commission estimates that in the whole of Brazil in 1971 land conflicts resulted in 20 deaths. Ten years later, in 1981, more than double that number (45 people) died in land conflicts. Conflict continued to escalate during the 1980s. In the five years between 1980 and 1984 there were 279 deaths in land conflicts. In the next five years, from 1985 to 1989, deaths totalled 488. And the tragic figures for deaths fail to give the whole picture. Over the period 1985 to 1989 there were 2,973 land conflicts. The extent of land under dispute totalled over three quarters of a million square kilometres. And over two million people were involved. To put this another way, during those five years some 16 Brazilians in every thousand were disputing ownership of almost 9 per cent of the national territory (an area almost equal to Britain and France together).

THE STRUGGLE FOR LAND

3

To journey in north-east Brazil from the coast into the interior is to cross a series of zones which are climatic and, consequently, socio-economic. The fertile coastal strip belongs to sugar cane, mile after mile of it. It is an area of large estates – small farmers have long since been squeezed out. Sugar provided the initial basis for the rise of an agricultural elite – an oligarchy – in Brazil in the colonial period. Cattle ranching developed along with sugar, providing beef and leather to the estates. The importance of sugar declined in the second half of the seventeenth century. Sugar made a big come-back in the 1970s after the oil crisis made it economic to run cars on sugar alcohol. Today, there are more sugar estates than ever.

Farther inland, the good agricultural land gives way to stonier, sandier soil. This is one of the last bastions of the small farmer. There are little houses by the roadside, some in good shape with neat flowered gardens around, others more dilapidated, with their roofs sagging under the weight of the heavy tiles, as if they were drooping in the heat of the midday sun. Further on in the arid interior known as the Sertão, the temperature rises steeply. Here the soils are poor and drought is common. People have to compete with cattle to scratch a meagre living. The roadside verges become peppered with small plots of crops – maize and beans. These are cultivated by landless people, who know that they are unlikely to be evicted from these narrow strips of Federal land between the asphalt and the first farm fence. Even this most basic and precarious existence is possible only in areas where there are no cattle-ranches whose wandering animals munch their way along the roadsides and through unfenced plots.

This chapter examines the plight of the rural poor in north-east Brazil – the sugar workers, the small farmers, and the landless. Here, in one of the richest economies in the world, small farmers are dying because of the greed of the rich farmers. There is landlessness and land conflict, because land that could support people is given over to cattle and sugar cane. And deforestation to clear more land for ranching is causing drought that has brought some communities to the edge of destruction.

DROUGHT

An overcast rainy day is a gloomy one for city people of the First World. For the farmers of the drought-stricken interior of Brazil's north-east, rain means a good day. One popular song in the north-eastern state of Paraiba goes, *"May a messenger from God bring me clothes, a hat and rain."*

Vertente – a community on the edge of death

The community of Vertente, near the town of Alagoa Grande in Paraiba, has always had it hard. Sixty families live there, squeezed on to five hectares of land. A black community, descendants of African slaves, they were already second-class citizens. The 1990 drought brought them to the edge of death. Their banana trees were dry, fragile, and cracking. Many had already fallen. The children were pot-bellied with hunger, large lifeless eyes staring from faces so gaunt that they already appeared elderly. Many had ear and eye infections. One man was so hungry that he staggered as he walked, with his eyes out of focus as if he were drunk. In April 1990, no one had been able to afford beans since January. Many people were able to eat only every few days.

Even in good years they only just make enough to feed themselves. There is nothing left over for clothes or medicines. The community has the highest levels of child mortality in the region. They have survived till now on their bananas, their few animals, small plots of maize and manioc on rented land, and casual labour in the sugar plantations. They used to wait by the roadside for the trucks that came to hire day labourers. But now the trucks don't come. And now they don't have the energy to work. Even getting water is a major task. They have to go to the top of the hill to a spring which yields water only drop by drop. It can take four hours to fill a pot.

Children in Vertente, Paraiba state, dancing to the music of the village band. (Jenny Matthews/ Oxfam)

They still play their music, slowly and with effort; but not sadly, *"because tomorrow we might have coffee"*. As the men play a *ciranda*, a song of happiness, the children, with their sad old faces, circle slowly, dancing to the music. It is like a religious service rather than a performance, reflecting perhaps the roots of their Afro-Brazilian culture.

The community had desperately hoped for short-term food aid from the local authorities. But, though a state of emergency was declared in other zones, they were by-passed. The men were forced to leave their families and migrate to the coast to look for work. To ensure the long-term future of their community, the people of Vertente want some land they can cultivate. The Rural Workers' Union (STR) of Alagoa Grande, supported by Oxfam, has been helping them to get organised as a community, to go to the local authorities for help in claiming land.

Drought and deforestation

The drought seems, at least in part, to be a man-made phenomenon. There was sustained drought in the first half of the 1980s. The rains returned in 1986, but, since then, the amount of rainfall has gone down year by year. The cane season in 1989 lasted only four months. And what little rainfall there is has become less and less predictable, making it impossible for farmers to plan their planting. Antonio Alves, the secretary of the Rural Workers' Union of Pirpirituba, has noticed the changes: *"The climate really began to change four years ago. The rains have been coming late. This year* [1990] *it began only at the end of April. And the amount of rainfall is less. In past years everyone would plant at Easter and have maize, beans, manioc, vegetables, rice and sweet potatoes for the feast of St John. This year there will be nothing."*

Antonio believes that the change in climate has been caused by deforestation. Until the Portuguese settlers came and began to chop down the trees, the forested Atlantic coast did not suffer from drought. Antonio has seen deforestation cause drought in Pirpirituba in his lifetime:

> *"There used to be a lot of trees around here – fruit trees, mangoes, Brazil nuts. This is the traditional vegetation. Now they've been cut down for cane and for cattle-grazing. This began in 1970. The only land we can get is on the tops of hills. All the good irrigated lowland is planted to cane. Once cane has been planted, or grass, it never goes back to agriculture. The cattle are there and eat the crops. Grass and cattle drive people out. And they're changing the climate."*

SHOWDOWN AT CARVED MOUNTAIN

Even in the arid Sertão there is violent conflict over the scarce land, with cattle ranchers trying to take over the land by theft, fraud and violent eviction.

In 1987 the homesteading farmers of Carved Mountain (Serra Talhada) in Pernambuco state realised a dream. After 16 years of range war with the big cattle barons, they have a fence to protect their crops from free-ranging cattle. Oxfam helped the farmers' organisation, the Serra Talhada Rural Workers' Union, that led the campaign for the fence.

(John Magrath/Oxfam)

The tabletop bulk of Carved Mountain dominates the municipality to which it gives its name. The arid land stretching away at its foot provides a meagre living to 5,000 homesteading families. They live in scattered communities of simple houses – most no more than a parlour, a bedroom, and a kitchen with a storeroom for harvested crops.

Overshadowing their lives were ten big cattle-ranching families. One homesteader, Antonio Nunez Ferreira Neto, remembers their desperation: *"Most of us live by the sweat of our brows, growing crops on little parcels of land. A handful of people farm cattle – 5, 10, 50 or 100 head. Always the cattle used to be roaming free. We'd plant our crops and the animals would come and eat them. We'd have to plant again, but we wouldn't get such a good yield because we'd missed the season. By the end of the year we wouldn't have enough to eat or enough to sell."*

For these subsistence farmers of the already arid north-east, it was like living through a permanent drought. The cattle barons simply laughed when hungry farmers turned up at their fancy homes looking for redress. *"They said it was our fault for not fencing"*, said Juvenal Rodriguez da Silva, an elder statesman of his community. *"They never used to think about fencing their 200 or 300 hectares. They would expect us to fence our tiny plots."*

Carving out a living on the edge of survival, the farmers did not have the money to fence their land. Some of these plots were smaller than the average British back garden, so divided and subdivided had the scarce land become. Many plots, because of this subdivision, were incredibly long and narrow. It did not make sense to fence them. Share-cropping was the only answer, as Antonio recalled: *"The only way out was to rent fenced land from the landowners. And they'd charge a rent of one part in four, or one in three, even half of our crop. But they'd never pay us rent for their cattle grazing on our land."*

Since they couldn't get justice individually, the farmers began to hold meetings together. Under the banner of the Rural Workers' Union they lobbied the mayor and the town council for a municipal law requiring the cattlemen to fence in their herds. At the beginning, Antonio remembers: *"We used to go down to the mayor's office to press our case. But the rich would turn up with their money, and that would be that. When the union started, we had someone to take up our case."*

At first the cattle barons were not worried. They had the council sewn up. But as the farmers gained support, they started trying to sabotage the meetings, telling farmers they'd been cancelled, or holding parties on the same day, with free food and cane liquor. Then in 1979 it looked as if the union had mustered enough support in the council to get a law passed. Tension was running high. The cattlemen brought in the gunmen. The union president, Raimundo Félix da Silva, was murdered. Raimundo's death, coupled with the severe drought of 1979-1984 when harvests were small anyway, took the momentum out of the struggle.

The union had to rethink and reorganise. One of the lessons of 1979 was how easy it was to decapitate the movement by killing the leaders. So they began to pass responsibility down the line to committees in the local communities. And within the union they began to rotate posts, so that no-one should become indispensable.

In 1982 a new mayor was elected, promising to campaign for a fence, but he didn't deliver on his promises. João Augusto commented cynically: *"You always hear people on the radio talking about supporting rural workers, especially when it comes up to 15 November* [election time]. *But after the elections you don't hear anything more about rural workers. But the union never stops talking about them."*

The union continued to lobby. By 1985 they had the support of five out of the nine councillors and two of the three local priests. The town council finally passed a fencing law in 1986, according to which the municipality agreed to provide materials and the farmers the labour for putting a fence round 10,000 hectares of agricultural land. At this point, hired gunslingers began to terrorise the farmers. Violence erupted as the people began work on the fence. One of the most bizarre episodes occurred when a cattle baron hired three gunmen to kill nine local activists. They were to be paid £4 for each murder. When the gunslingers saw how organised the people were, they raised their price to £40 a killing. The cattle rancher refused, and they holed up in a vacant house while they negotiated. People got word of this and surrounded the house. They began talking to the gunslingers, who complained bitterly to their intended victims about their employer's intransigence. The end was bloodless. The gunslingers simply left town.

As the fence grew, fence posts were torn out during the night, the wire was cut, and crops growing near the fence were burned. The gunmen menaced the workers and laid ambushes for them. Adelmo da Souza Lima, a local activist, was shot dead in February 1987 in an ambush. But in the end the fence went up.

Conflict simmered for a while afterwards. Cattle which were found inside the fence were shot, or given poison, or had dogs set on them. The cattle barons retaliated by putting down poisoned meat, killing some of the dogs.

But now the farmers are harvesting twice as much as before. Juvenal Rodriguez da Silva used to plant 10 *tarefas* (about 3 hectares) of maize and beans, and even then he couldn't afford to fence all of it in, and he would regularly lose part of his crop to cattle. Now he plants 20 *tarefas* and harvests all of it. Antonio gestures happily at a pile of harvested beans drying in his storeroom and says: *"For you from outside this may look like crude food. But let me tell you these are good beans. This is what we have now."*

The lesson of Serra Talhada is that grassroots education and involvement were the basis for a successful campaign. In a neighbouring municipality, rural workers managed to get a similar law passed, but with the absence of local involvement, it was not enforced.

In Serra Talhada, as in many other parts of rural Brazil, the Rural Workers' Unions (STRs) provide one of the few forms of mutual support available to the small farmers, and one of the few institutions that give them a voice in society.

THE PLIGHT OF THE SUGAR WORKERS

But it is sugar rather than cattle which has taken most of the good land out of foodcrop production. The sugar workers of the north-east are among the most exploited in the country. Even if they are lucky enough to have a little land to farm, it is generally not enough to live on. They have to work in the cane fields. And the whims of the sugar estate owners are still law.

Maria Jose Trajano da Silva is a cane worker in Alagoa Grande in Paraiba. She works from 5.00 a.m. to 5.00 p.m. with two hours for lunch. Her pay amounts to about £1.80 a week. Men get about £2.40 a week for exactly the same work of planting and weeding. Cane workers are paid piece-rates – between 35 and 70 pence (depending on the estate) for a two-day task. A kilo of beans (part of the staple diet) costs 60 pence. So, it takes them about two days' work to pay for a kilo of beans. It takes three days to buy two kilos of sugar or a tin of cooking oil. In the period between harvests, work is hard to come by. And frequent drought makes things worse.

In 1990, there was a severe drought. Though the mile after mile of sugar-cane monoculture looked green, underneath everything was dying. Estates that normally hired 30 people were now hiring ten. The sugar mills were not working. And the drought coincided with the drastic anti-inflationary package of the incoming government of Fernando Collor. There was little money in circulation, and the sugar estates were cutting back even further on employment. Merchants, trying to beat the government's price freeze, had taken their beans off the market and were stockpiling them. Hungry sugar workers had been breaking into food stores. Their situation was desperate. Their only hope was for Paraiba to be officially declared a disaster zone, so that they qualified for Federal aid. For Maria Jose, *"There is nothing. We are eating only manioc flour. There are no beans to buy now. My children don't like it. I have four children. The hunger is tremendous. I go to work with only a cigarette. I don't eat."*

She lives in a tied cottage and has no land. There are 35 people living on the estate; four of the workers are women. Unlike full-time workers elsewhere, who have a right to a fixed annual bonus, equivalent to a thirteenth month of salary, the cane workers' bonus is fixed by the whim of the estate owner. Around Alagoa Grande it can vary from 60 pence for women and £1.20 for men, to £2.40 for women and £3.60 for men. They have asked for wage increases, but the landowner just told them to hand in their machetes and leave if they didn't like the conditions.

And conditions can be even worse elsewhere. In Triunfo, in the neighbouring state of Pernambuco, the mills are small-time and most sugar is grown by share-croppers rather than on plantations. The mill-owners are often the landlords too. They charge share-croppers half their sugar harvest in rent and then another tenth of their sugar for milling it. Elerio Nogueira da Lima works in a sugar mill in Triunfo. He is a *serrador:* he feeds the cane-crushing machine, one of the most dangerous jobs. All of the jobs are done by men. Women and children do not work in the mills. The *serrador* earns the most money because of the danger of losing a limb to the crusher. Asked if he would rather work with properly protected equipment and earn a little less, Elerio was emphatic: No way! The dangerous jobs are much sought after, because of the little bit of extra money they carry. He earns two pence a tray, and produces 43 or 44 trays a day. This is around 85 pence a day. He has a wife and five children. He says he just gets by. Elerio works from 1.00 in the morning until 4.00 or 5.00 in the afternoon. He is home by 6.00 or 6.30, having had lunch and supper in the mill. He goes to sleep at 8.00 or 8.30. If he can sleep through till midnight, he's happy. But if he wakes up for any reason, he doesn't dare go back to sleep for fear of losing worktime and pay.

Working on a sugar cane plantation. Piece-work rates can be as low as 30 pence a day. (Frances Rubin/ Oxfam)

Because of conditions like these, the Rural Workers' Unions in areas like Alagoa Grande and Triunfo have been helping sugar workers fight for better conditions.

THE RURAL WORKERS' UNIONS

There is a local branch of the Serra Talhada Rural Workers' Union (STR) in Triunfo. Its headquarters is situated in a narrow cobbled street, shaded by trees bearing orange blossom. It occupies a long narrow hall on the first floor. A row of slatted wooden benches faces a table, ready for a meeting. A crucifix hangs above a blackboard, which still bears the assembly details for the First of May demonstration. In a corner stands a packing case containing a diesel engine and an antique slow-speed dentist's drill.

Demonstrations and dental care – these are the two faces of Brazilian rural unions, the new and the old. Unions here have a very different history from those in Europe: they were created not by the workers, but by the state. The Rural Workers' Unions (STRs), like all Brazilian unions, were originally set up under the military government in the 1930s under Mussolini's model rules. They were intended as a means of keeping an eye on workers. By law, every worker is supposed to pay a day's wages every year to finance the state-imposed union structure. Every town or rural area has to have a separate union for each industry or sector, which makes for a proliferation of unions. The state gave the unions something to offer members by making them responsible for pensions and medical benefits.

Although the 1988 Constitution has ended state control over unions' internal affairs, perhaps 80 per cent of STRs still confine themselves to these functions. Activists who are trying to turn their unions into modern representative structures say that the leaderships still represent the interests of the bosses. Zé Preá, a charismatic leader of an STR in Pernambuco, describes the bosses' reactions to attempts to democratise the unions: *"They kill them. There have been many deaths in the area of people trying to create proper unions. They fiddle elections as well. They pay their supporters' arrears, and confiscate the union cards of people they think are going to vote against them, on pain of losing their jobs."*

Penha Nascimento holding a copy of her life-story. (Jenny Matthews/ Oxfam)

One of those who gave their lives for her work in the Rural Unions was Margarida Maria Alves, the legendary president of the Alagoa Grande Union. She received constant death threats. Finally, on 12 August 1983, during a campaign for higher wages for sugar workers, she was assassinated. Penha Nascimento, with her husband Zé Horacio, carries on Margarida's work in the Union. She has become almost as well-known as Margarida. In a pamphlet, Penha gave a moving description of her life.

In 1984, a year after Margarida's death, cane workers throughout Paraiba staged their first strike. They won some improvements in pay and conditions, and began to standardise rates of pay across the estates. By 1990 the unions in Paraiba were able to provide the cane workers with a table of payments by weight and little portable scales that can weigh a 20 kilo load of cane. This allows them to tell whether they are being short-changed for their piece-work labour at harvest time. But there is still a long way to go before they reap any benefits from Brazil's 'white gold'.

Penha's story

I am the daughter of a rural woman, who left the countryside and went to the city of João Pessoa, to be a domestic ... after three years ... I was born. My mother ... took me to my grandparents' house. ... she threw me on their laps and went to work and live in a nightclub. This was the only work she could get, to be able to survive. ...

When I was 12 my mother came back... She had TB and was vomiting a lot of blood. She was dying, needing help. But the landlords didn't let her stay, because they said that their children would catch the disease. So she had to go and die there, alone, in the nightclub.

I stayed with my grandparents. I began to revolt against the life of the bosses, because they didn't let her come and die near me. ... But I thought that this was the way God wanted it, that God had made poor and rich. My grandparents couldn't afford to send me to secondary school. And I began to work at just seven years old.

When Zé Horacio came to Alagoa Grande, I was only just eight. He was about 12. ... When we fell in love I was hardly 10... And we ended up marrying in 1963. ..

When we got married, Zé Horacio was working harvesting aloes. He would go out on Monday and come home on Saturday. Afterwards, he moved to working in the sugar cane fields, loading the cane lorries. We had many difficulties raising our children. At times we couldn't afford to feed ourselves properly, to buy clothes and to send the kids to school. It was a very hard struggle. Each day we suffered more. ...

Today I have six children. The youngest has health problems because of the violence, caused by the impact of the death of Margarida. She and Margarida's sons were great friends, they played together, and at the time she [Margarida] was assassinated, she was hardly four. She is still afraid when I go to a meeting or an appointment, and she keeps asking me whether there will be bosses there, when I'm coming back, etc. Whenever I go on a long trip, I always have to call her. When I am able to phone her she often cries. ...

In 1972 I joined the Alagoa Grande Rural Workers' Union. Zé Horacio had joined in 1969. Margarida was treasurer of the Union...

In 1980 Zé Horacio ... had become secretary of the Union, [which was now] led by Margarida ... In the struggle, together with Margarida, we shared a lot, up to the day she was assassinated.

On Margarida's last night, the 11th August 1983, we were together, sleeping in Guarabira, ... where we were at a meeting...

That day Margarida told me about all the violence she was suffering, all the threats the bosses were making. Sadly we weren't given time to denounce everything she told me. On the twelfth, we parted in the morning, and at 5.30 in the afternoon she was barbarously assassinated.

Her death happened while she was leading a salary campaign. We were demanding holidays, payment of the 'thirteenth month' [a normal bonus in Brazil], and signed workcards [guaranteeing state benefits]... This is why she was killed. She died because she was struggling against the interests of the bosses, the big landowners...

It wasn't easy carrying on the struggle. There were a lot of pressures. There were many threatening letters, which began to appear under the Union door. Things like: "Margarida is gone already, who will be next?" ... Despite all the pressures, we went ahead. Zé Horacio took over the leadership of the Union and we advanced in organisation.

"I began to work at just seven years old."

FIGHTING FOR WOMEN'S RIGHTS

The Rural Workers' Unions have helped improve conditions for small farmers and sugar workers. But other forms of mutual aid are important too. Women's needs are often ignored or seen as less important by the men who run most of the unions. And so during the 1980s a women's movement began to take shape alongside the union structures.

In some cases the women's movement has fought for equal treatment between men and women. In Pernambuco state the women's movement began as a response by women to the drought of the early 1980s. Women are specially affected by drought, because they are responsible for feeding the family. But the state government, which was supplying emergency aid to the men during the drought, denied it to women. The women organised to demand equal treatment.

The women's movement is also trying to encourage more women to play an active part in the Rural Workers' Unions. This means helping women to gain confidence, and it also means persuading reluctant men to accept the women. In the 200 communities served by the Serra Talhada STR only four had women union representatives. Vanete de Almeida, the union full-timer, believes: *"You can't change a centuries-old tradition overnight. We have to change the consciousness of the men, the women and the children. Sometimes even the leaders who should support us have problems understanding."* Vanete is beginning to promote women-only meetings. The aim is not to create a parallel women's movement, but to give women confidence to raise their own special demands within the union.

In December 1987 the Serra Talhada STR helped to organise the first state-wide meeting of women rural workers. The four demands were land to work; equal pay for equal work; a campaign for the unionisation and participation of women; and a just social security. (Women have no social security rights except through their husbands.)

Penha Nascimento of the Alagoa Grande STR argues that women must also have the opportunity to put their own special demands on the unions' agenda:

> *"In this union the women are used during pickets and in the occupation of land. So the women are accepted in the union. But it has not opened up the space for women to talk of their particular needs... things like a creche, rights to social services, equal pay, maternity leave. Women must first discover that they have these rights, then explain them to the union, then get the union to fight for them as its demands. Women and men must work together on formulating the union's demands. For example, there are places where a lot of pesticides are used. This has an effect on pregnant women. They have to struggle* [for the union to take this up as an issue] *first as women. Whether we do this by forming separate women's groups depends on the area – women's groups are formed where the men don't accept these demands or exclude women from the leadership."*

Unlike the unions, the women's movement brings together people from different sectors – rural and urban. In Paraiba women responded to the assassination of the union leader Margarida by naming their movement after her: the Movement of Working Women of the Brejo, Margarida Maria Alves. Its slogan is "Daisies [*margaridas*] from the blood of Margarida". It was formed in 1984, with support from Oxfam, and played a leading role in organising the first state-wide Congress of women in 1986. This meeting brought together domestic workers, washerwomen, factory workers, teachers and rural workers. It allowed the growing organisation of women to discuss what they wanted to press for in the forthcoming Constituent Assembly.

The movement operates in almost 20 municipalities of Paraiba, involving almost 7,000 women. It is led by a group of 12 women representing the teachers, domestic servants and agricultural workers of the area. Using techniques such as door-to-door canvassing, meetings and courses, they tackle issues including land rights, low salaries, lack of confidence, family relationships, exclusion from the unions, and domestic violence. They also develop leadership skills.

Lucia de Fatima Félix is a member of the women's movement. She is a school teacher in the rural community of Videl, earning only £8.50 a month. She works three hours a day in the school, and spends the rest of the day in the fields. She became involved with the women's movement in 1986, and began to draw other women in. Two years later six women made their first attempt to work some land together. They planted tomatoes, but the soil was not good enough for them and they died. Now they are trying again, growing manioc, sweet potatoes, beans and maize. They have dug a well, and Lucia has been on an alternative technology course to learn how to fertilise the land without chemicals.

But quite apart from any material benefits they may enjoy from working together is the mutual support they find. For Josefa Augusta de Souza, this is the real importance of the local women's group:

> *"Here there is a big problem – that men don't like women to go out to meetings. But we go all the same. I say 'I'm not going to cook your dinner. I'm off.' They are good when we come back. But many don't do anything at all in the house. I'm lucky. When I go to market my husband looks after the children and cooks – rice and beans at least. The husbands who help are those in the union, who are more in solidarity. It's good this organisation, because we have more defence. If there is a problem with a father or a brother or a husband, we know we are not alone."*

"It's good this organisation, because we know we are not alone."

ESPERANÇA – HOPE OF THE LANDLESS

For the growing number of people without land and work, there are only two solutions: migrate, or try to find and take over abandoned land. The Landless People's Movement is one response. It works by taking over unoccupied land. Esperança, which means *hope* in Portuguese, illustrates what happens.

Surrounded by parched desert fields, the Esperança farm is a crude encampment of houses made by stretching black polythene sheeting over low wood frames. In the centre is a makeshift flagpole, and in the wind whistling over the hillsides the red flag of the MST, the Landless People's Movement, snaps proudly. These are the landless people of Paraiba, people driven out by sugar and cattle. More than 500 people, representing 150 families, moved on to this 100-hectare farm at the end of 1989.

The MST, with funds from Oxfam, helps landless people gain access to land under Brazil's agrarian reform laws. The laws allowing the state to confiscate and redistribute idle land are honoured more in the breach than in reality. For the landless, the only option has become to move on to idle land and make it produce, hoping that by creating facts on the ground they can weather intimidation by local landed elites, and fight their way through the legal battles to get ownership of the land.

Rural social classes

Brazilians have very precise designations of the rural social classes in terms of their exact relationship to the land. There are landless rural workers, who work for a wage, either as temporary or permanent labour. Then there are *posseiros* (squatters), who occupy land to which they have no legal title. Finally there are different categories of those with land titles. The Brazilian concept of the *posseiro* defines a legal status rather different from the English word *squatter*. Unused land may be squatted, but the squatters have no rights until they have been on the land for a year and a day. At that point, if there is no dispute about the occupation, they acquire squatters' rights. After five years, squatters can apply to have their possession of the land legally recognised as ownership, and, if necessary, transfer the title. This is a rare outcome. What usually happens is evictions by the big landowners.

Some of the people in Esperança have returned to their original homes for survival, because there is no food on the farm. But others remain there to maintain their claim to the land, trying to coax a little manioc out of the dry earth and to fish in the rivers.

Maria do Carmo Marcenas is one of the six community leaders of Esperança. Her position is a testament to the strength of the women's movement in Paraiba. In Esperança the men do their share of cooking. Their rules are that the men have to help the women in the house, and the women work with the men in the fields. Maria do Carmo played a central part in the move on to the land:

Maria do Carmo Marcenas at home in Esperança. (Jenny Matthews/ Oxfam)

"We had a meeting, so we came as a group, organised. We took a collection, so that everyone who could afford it contributed money to get a ride in the trucks. We came on to the land in the night. We weren't frightened of anything, because there were a lot of us. I was prepared to confront anything to get land. The first thing we did was to make the houses. We had brought a few things from our old homes: a few plates, pans, a few beans."

"I was prepared to confront anything to get land."

Esperança was an abandoned farm, belonging to the father of a town councillor in the municipality of Esperança. The owner attempted to have them evicted by a court official. But the people are well-prepared to defend their land. As well as the court official, they have seen off ten policemen. There are look-outs posted day and night around the perimeter. When there is a threat, the children go in front, armed with sticks and stones, then the women behind them, then behind them the men, all armed with agricultural tools.

Josefa Leonardo dos Santos knows from bitter experience how important these preparations are. By the age of 30, she and her husband Edimilson had tried three times to get some land. She remembers how the police drove them out of an abandoned banana plantation in 1989:

"They were shooting, throwing gas bombs, beating us up. It caught fire where we were. Everyone ran. The police got hold of Edimilson to beat him up. Everyone else got away. I went back when I saw they had got my husband. They beat my children. They beat me too, beat me badly – I still have the marks on my shoulders and chest. They beat my husband, then they beat me, then they beat him again. They broke his arm. The police caught some other people along the roadside and cut them."

In Esperança they have been luckier, as Maria do Carmo remembers:

"In the first days nobody slept; everyone was on their guard, ready for an attack. When the police came with the paper to remove us, everyone sang songs about the Agrarian Reform and chanted the words of our movement: 'Occupy, Resist, Produce'. The police stopped and negotiated with us. They were surprised that there were so many people ready to confront them. They weren't ready for it."

Now the government has promised that they will be given the land, and people have come there from all over the region. José Neris Rodriguez da Silva is definitely there to stay. He has already built a permanent house instead of the polythene tent. Built of stones with a tile roof, it is home to him, his wife and their seven children. He has planted beans and squash. He says:

"People have suffered here. The children are hungry and thirsty. I haven't eaten for seven days. We came here for land. We didn't come to get rich. People were born from the land and must live from it. I can't read and write. How can I fight against the landowner's lawyers? But we have a lawyer from the movement. I have been in the union for 14 years. I worked for a landowner for 20 years and then he just threw me off the land. He could do that because he was powerful."

For people who have not been so lucky as the community at Esperança, the lure of a new life in the Amazon has beckoned. This is described in the next chapter.

4 COLONISTS

The highway running down the Tocantins river in the eastern Amazon is one of many new roads that have been bored through the forest. Along the roadside, mile after mile of devastated forest: blackened skeletons of trees, cattle grazing amid the tree stumps, the rainforest visible only distantly on the horizon. Wholesale burning is used to clear the land. A few forest giants survive, towering bleak and lone against the sun. All are leafless, dying from lack of the nutrients which the other species used to pump back into the soil.

The land in the north has been taken over by the big agro-industrial companies, some foreign-owned, such as the Dutch company Denpasa, and others Brazilian. They grow oil palms, peppercorns and other tropical crops. Farther south, the land turns drier. This is the land of the colonists, small farmers. The cattle are scrawnier. Here the thin and fragile soil has already given up most

New highway through the rainforest, Rondônia. (Tony Gross/ Oxfam)

of its riches, sucked dry in a few frantic years of colonisation. There are more small homesteads. But also there are more abandoned houses, their skeletons bleaching in the sun, each the last testament to the failure of some settler's hopes and dreams.

In other places there are little embryo communities, clusters of huts where a group of people searching for land has just stopped by the roadside and begun to put down roots. More communities are spreading out from the road, following the logging trails that lead into the forest. It is easy to think of Brazil as a giant ant run, with streams of people crossing the country from end to end, searching for gold, searching for work, searching for land. The roadside communities in a matter of months swell into hamlets. The logging trails become roads. The roads get paved. And in no time at all there are new cities in the forest.

"People who want to deforest Amazonia first design a road project, and with the road comes destruction, behind a mask called progress."

(Jaime da Silva Araujo, first President of the National Council of Rubber-Tappers.)

FALSE PROMISES

As new roads began to open up the Amazonian frontier, settlers poured in from the slums of the south and the arid lands of the north-east: poor people desperate for a new life. Whole families made the long journey in 'parrot lorries', which get their names not only because everyone perches like birds crammed together on narrow planks, but also because of a form of torture practised in the era of the military governments. The construction of the Belém-Brasilia highway in the 1960s improved access to land in the states of Pará and Goiás. Later road-building programmes in the 1970s opened up the more remote western states of Roraima, Rondônia and Acre.

Between 1960 and 1980 the population of Amazonia more than doubled – from 5,300,000 to 12,200,000. But this colonisation programme was a false promise based on a false premise: that the soils of the Amazon were fertile. The luxuriance of the rainforest had naturally prompted this idea from the moment in the sixteenth century when Orellana, the first European to reach the Amazon, had seen the Indians' cultivations of manioc, sweet potatoes and vegetables. Alfred Russell Wallace, co-author with Charles Darwin of the theory of evolution, who visited the Amazon in the middle of the last century, wrote:

> *"I fearlessly assert that here the primeval forest can be converted into rich pastureland, into cultivated gardens and orchards, containing every variety of produce, with half the labour, and, what is more important, in less than half the time than would be required at home."*[5]

The first Spanish and Portuguese explorers could not understand why the Indians of the Amazon valley rotated their plantations every three years. In their arrogance they attributed it to superstition, thinking this the only possible explanation of the labour involved. But the Indians knew, as the explorers did not, that the luxuriant growth of the rainforest grew on top of a virtual desert. The fecundity depends on the closed and self-maintaining ecosystem of the forest, storing nutrients in the living vegetation and producing new growth on the detritus of the old. Once the forest is cleared, the soil rapidly becomes sterile. The Indians were practising basic conservation.

"They had been brought up to consider land to be a gift of God, like rain and sunshine."

Manoel, a leader of peasant farmers in Itupiranga in the eastern Amazon, explains:

> *"After clearing the land and planting two or three times, the land isn't much good any more. They don't have any fertiliser. It's difficult to get technical help. So in the end, the farmer loses his harvest. Usually what happens then is that people lay down grass to graze cattle because they can't do much else. They may rent their land out for grazing, but generally they try and sell up. So the ranchers gradually agglomerate the small plots."*

One elderly man from the state of Bahia came to find land to work. Now he works in a saw-mill:

> *"We came in 1973. We were cheated. Some people came and made a lot of noise in Bahia. They told us life was good in Pará. They told us you could earn back in one hour the money you spent on the fare. So we came with other families in the lorry. When we arrived we didn't even have a house. We were just dumped under a tree in the mud. Now we're stuck here. People from as far away as Bahia never get back."*

LAND CONFLICT

The colonists' problems are created not just by the ecology of the region. Their most immediate problems are economic and political, caused by people, not by nature. Land values have soared in the Amazon, and big ranching interests have followed the settlers to the new frontier. Many families migrated to the Amazon because they had been uprooted from their land in the south or north-east by commercial crops such as coffee, sugar and soya. Now settlers find themselves being forced to move on again as ranchers drive them off their new land.

Often the wave of migration has been only a few years ahead of the companies. The settlers attempt to farm for a few years before they are bought out or violently evicted by big landowners. A recent study notes the way in which the peasant settlers from the north-east were unprepared culturally as well as economically for this unequal contest:

> *"In the beginning the peasants were particularly vulnerable to attempts to dislodge them. Many did not understand the concept of property in the modern world. As no one in their families had ever paid money for the land they tilled, they did not attribute value to the land itself, but only to the labour they had expended in clearing the forest and building their huts. However, although the peasant farmers were bewildered by the logic of capitalism, landowners understood all too well the values of the peasant world and frequently took cruel advantage of their ignorance. We often met baffled peasant farmers who had been offered what they had to admit was fair compensation for their crops, huts, barbed wire and so on; and yet they instinctively felt they had been tricked and deceived. They knew that they had lost something – their land – which was essential to their life. Yet, as they had been brought up to consider land to be a gift of God, like rain and sunshine, they did not immediately realise that they had indeed been robbed and that, in the modern world they were entering, land was a commodity to be bought and sold like sacks of rice."*[6]

Gateway to the Primavera estate, Rondônia. Beyond the fence: ravaged rainforest.
(Tony Gross/ Oxfam)

Where the smallholders refuse to be bought out, the ranchers in many cases take the land by outright robbery, known as *grilagem*: they simply fence in the land and declare it to be theirs. Anyone on the land is violently expelled. Some large landowners are said to have created private militias to clear the land. Etelvinho Porto works for the Catholic Church's Pastoral Land Commission (CPT) in Paragominas in the state of Pará. He knows about land robbery from his own experience. He came to Pará in 1968 when he was 14, with his parents and ten brothers and sisters:

> *"The vision my father had was that this was a place where you could get land, work, money. He settled on five different pieces of land, but now he has nothing. Every time we settled a piece of land, someone who said he was the owner would appear and chuck us off."*

Now he works to help the small farmers defend their rights. Often the legal status of the landowners' titles is dubious. Etelvinho talks of 'flying titles':

> *"We call them 'flying titles' because they are used for several different pieces of land. It's difficult to prove that they are different areas, because we're talking about huge areas of the jungle. The gunmen are always guarding these areas. It's not just any old person who's going to go and check out whether it's true, because of the danger. Even people from INCRA* [the Institute for Colonisation and Land Reform] *have been threatened. On one estate near here, INCRA people were forbidden to go in."*

Many agricultural workers in Paragominas have turned for help to the CPT, which works alongside the Rural Workers' Union. These two institutions (both partly funded by Oxfam) provide an advisory service, informing rural workers about government policy, and encouraging them to work together to find

"If we have two weeks when no one is killed, we reckon it is a good fortnight."

solutions to their problems. The CPT also offers technical advice on issues like organic composting and pesticide use. Oxfam contributes the salary of an agricultural technician. The CPT team visits outlying communities within an enormous 27,000 square kilometre area and holds meetings, outlining the impact of the big development projects, encouraging community initiatives such as communal gardens. The team also helps with the legalities of land titles and with marketing of produce, such as peppers and the *guaraná* fruit.

Workers for the CPT have been threatened. In 1986 two members of the CPT team were forced to leave the area after receiving telephoned death threats. They claimed they came from the right-wing UDR (Rural Democratic Union), financed by the big ranchers. Small farmers and the remaining indigenous people face constant threats to their land. Etelvinho Porto says: *"If we have two weeks when no one is killed, in land conflict or whatever, we reckon it is a good fortnight."*

Today, much of the land in Pará is held by large ranches belonging to national and multinational companies. Most of the small farmers have been pushed into the backwoods or have joined the pool of cheap labour for the cattle ranches. Very few people are employed as permanent wage labour on the ranches as cowboys or such-like. Most wage labourers are recruited by middlemen for temporary labour gangs at below-minimum wages of 60-70p a day. These gangs clear the forest, often being kept in conditions of semi-slavery, working from 4.30 a.m. to 2.00 or 3.00 in the afternoon. They are forced to buy shoddy goods at inflated prices from the company stores, and debt as well as coercion by private guards serves to keep them at their task.

WHICH FUTURE?

5

The conflict over land in Brazil is a struggle over the different visions of what development can mean – visions which are different economically, ecologically and socially. This chapter examines what lies behind them.

THE GENERALS' VISION

The military governments that ruled between 1964 and 1985 had a very clear vision of development. The generals, together with a small technocratic elite, had set out to turn Brazil into the major world power that its size and riches merited. They aimed to industrialise the country, and to open up the Amazon frontier. The Amazon was opened up according to a plan that was at the same time military, political and economic. In the words of a member of the Marabá-based ecological information and training group, CEPASP:

> *"In the 1970s there was a difficult land question in the north-east. The* [government] *didn't want to divide up the land of the colonels* [a term for the powerful]. *There was also the whole question of national security: repopulating the Amazon frontier to defend national sovereignty. So they started bringing them up here in lorries. There was a rush to come here. People who had land in the south sold up there for a lot of money and came up north to make a new life. They could buy big areas with a small amount of money. So the conflicts started. They thought there was a land without people, but there were people here. They didn't necessarily have title to the land – they were people native to the region. There were nuts, there was rubber, there was gold here, and people had come a long time before.* [The new] *people cut down the forest, laid down grass and made grazing land. They were called the pioneers, people who had come to develop Amazonia!"*

The political motive

In the 1960s pressure on land by the big estates in the south and the north-east was growing. Life became impossible for the subsistence farmers. By 1950 over half the farms in the north-east were smaller than 10 hectares. Ten years later these micro-farms made up almost two-thirds of farms in the region. They were

For every half ton of forest vegetation cleared, one hamburger is produced.

simply too small to sustain the families trying to live on them. Unemployment and underemployment in the countryside reached 37 per cent.

The possibility of land reform was blocked by the powerful vested interests of the landowners. The Amazon was seen as a safety-valve to siphon off the political pressure. The government promoted the idea of the Amazon as a 'land without people for people without land'.

The military motive

The generals feared that in the vast and largely forgotten interior of the continent lay a deep threat to national security. In Amazonia, Brazil borders Colombia, Venezuela, Peru and Bolivia, as well as the small territories of Guyana, Surinam and French Guiana. Military strategists feared that Brazil would lose territory, unless these frontiers were secured by populating the Amazon.

Ironically, the rubber-tappers provided a strong spur to this fear. In the late nineteenth century, as rubber-tappers spread out through the Amazon, they crossed the frontier into what was then the territory of Acre, disputed with Bolivia. This led to the 1902-1903 war with Bolivia in which Brazil annexed Acre, and the country reached its present geographical limits. This experience has etched itself deeply on the institutional psyche of the Brazilian army, who have also not forgotten that the United States threatened to intervene militarily on Bolivia's side in the Acre war.

The military established a network of roads and frontier posts along Brazil's borders. Colonists were brought in to populate these posts. This has created particular problems for the Indian peoples. For the Indians living in these regions, borders meant nothing; many nations, such as the Yanomami, straddle the frontier. But the military elements of the government regarded them as a security problem which took priority over discussion of any rights to territory. Along the northern borders, 150,000 kilometres are under military control. Here indigenous colonies are planned for the Indians.

The economic motive

But the generals wanted to do more than just populate the Amazon: they wanted to develop it. They saw a choice between two different ways in which the territory could be occupied – that of the big companies, which they saw as modern, and that of the small peasant farmers, which they saw as backward. There was a conflict between the economic motive and the political motive of providing land for the landless. And very shortly the government started to give priority for agriculture to the big companies, who could pay for the land and, in the minds of the planners, 'develop' it.

So incentives were offered to the big companies to ensure that Amazonia was occupied in what the government saw as a modern and productive way. From 1973 car, steel and food-packaging magnates were encouraged by means of credit and tax 'holidays' to diversify and invest, especially in cattle ranching. Companies were offered tax holidays for up to 17 years, grants totalling up to three-quarters of the value of their investment, and cheap credit (effectively at negative rates of interest, given Brazil's serious inflation levels). On top of this,

Roadworks in progress: the construction of the highway from Rio Branco (Acre) to Porto Velho (Rondônia). (Tony Gross/ Oxfam)

the government provided vital infrastructure in the form of the road-building programme which allowed the companies to move their produce to market. All of this added together has meant healthy profits for the individual investor. Even unproductive land has been a profitable investment.

Indeed, much of the land has not been put to use. Government agencies have been satisfied by the appearance rather than the reality of development. Often, the real motive for investment has been land speculation rather than ranching. Many of the new landowners do no more than clear the fringes of their lands and graze a few cows in order to convince government inspectors that they are using the land productively. As a result it is not surprising that Amazonia remains a net *importer* of beef, according to a recent study (Hecht and Cockburn 1989).

The ecological consequences

The government incentives were given in vain. The big landowners, like the small farmers, soon discovered the poor quality of much of the Amazonian land. This type of use of the forest is doomed ecologically and economically. Calculations suggest that for every half ton of forest vegetation cleared, one hamburger is produced. On the same amount of land required to produce one hamburger – six-and-a-quarter square metres – a Brazil-nut tree produces each year 30 kilograms of nuts, with a protein value of 21 per cent. One steer, which requires more than a hectare of land, produces only 22 kilograms of meat, with a protein rating of 19 per cent.

Studies in the state of Acre show that the soils reach maximum profitability at five years of use, both for livestock production and agriculture. After about 15 years, they are no longer profitable for livestock or agriculture. Traditional extraction (rubber-tapping and Brazil-nut harvesting), on the other hand, maintains a constant self-reproducing level of profitability.

Gomercindo Clovis Garcia Rodriguez works for the Centro de Trabalhadores da Amazonia (the Amazonia Workers' Centre) in the state of Acre. He is nervous and jerky, his thin hands in continual agitation as he speaks – brushing back the sweep of long black hair that falls into his eyes, gesturing, emphasising. He clicks his fingers as he reels off the figures:

> *"This land can produce 200 kilos of meat per hectare per year. At today's price of 57 pence per kilo, this means a return of £114 per hectare per year. That's without taking into account the costs of clearing the land, medicines for the cattle, etc. But from Brazil nuts you can easily get £85-114. And that's without any additional cost. But capitalism is only interested in quick profit. So they take their quick profit and go on to another area."*

The scale of destruction in Acre has already been immense: 30 per cent of the municipality of Xapurí was deforested between 1977 and 1984. This means 180,000 rubber trees destroyed, 80,000 Brazil-nut trees, and 120,000 hardwoods.

In the early 1970s there was an opportunity to take a different approach to the opening up of the Amazon. In 1966-67 the Institute for Colonisation and Land Reform (INCRA) surveyed land ownership in the region. Of 487 million hectares, only 124 million were in private ownership. Legally, most of the land belonged to the state, which could dispose of it as it wished. It would therefore have been possible to meet the demands of most Indian groups for recognition of their traditional lands. On the remainder of the land, it would have been possible to grant title to small farmers. This would not only have made good social sense, it would also have made good economic sense.

This is not to romanticise the small colonist. The pattern of land use by the small farmer is also deeply destructive. The small farmers clear-cut the forest, destroying many valuable trees. They farm the cleared patches to exhaustion, lay down grass, and then move on to clear another patch, rather than fertilising the soil. They increase the rate of soil erosion by planting their crops in straight lines. They use the land poorly, partly because of lack of adequate support services and lack of credit for inputs like fertilisers. But they do this partly also in accordance with the topsy-turvy rationality of Amazonian development. Many know they will not be able to keep their land; they will be forced to sell up to the ranchers. And the more of their plot they have cleared, the higher the price it will fetch.

An INCRA study in 1971 found that the existing pattern of land tenure was inefficient: the small peasant farms were too small for development, and the large farms were unproductive. So they recommended a land reform, transferring land to the squatters and small farmers. The state government of Rondônia found in a 1969 survey that small farmers were more productive than large farmers: at that time, small farms formed only 35 per cent of the occupied land, but they grew 96 per cent of the state's agricultural produce; in contrast, large farms formed 65 per cent of the occupied land but contributed only 4 per cent of the output.

But the decision was influenced by power politics rather than rationality. The large companies reaped the benefits. Rondônia, for example, has seen the greatest proportionate growth of any part of Amazonia. In the single decade between 1970 and 1980 its population more than quadrupled. But the form of growth led to uncontrolled conflict between peasant settlers, land speculators, cattle ranchers, tin prospectors, and Indians. An unknown number of Uru-Weu-Wau-Wau Indians living on the edge of the BR-364 highway were massacred. In a huge and continuing sell-off, the state lands of Amazonia are being transformed into the type of private assets least likely to make a contribution to development.

A DIFFERENT VISION: THE EXTRACTIVE RESERVES

The rubber-tappers have an alternative. They do not want to stop development, but to develop in a way that is sustainable and protects their communities and the forest. In the words of Chico Mendes:

> *"The rubber-tappers aren't saying that nobody should lay a finger on the Amazon. No. We've got our own proposals for organising production. The rubber-tappers and the Indians have always grown their subsistence crops, but they've never threatened the existence of the forest. It's the deforestation carried out by the big landowners to open up pasture for their cattle that is threatening the forest."*

At the heart of the rubber-tappers' vision is the idea of creating 'extractive reserves'. Rather like the idea of Indian reservations, the rubber-tappers want areas of the forest set aside for the exclusive use of extractivists working in the traditional sustainable way. Antonio Pinheiro, a father of five, feels:

> *"Ours is a good life. The Brazil-nut and rubber trees feed my children. These* fazendeiros *just want to fell the forest. If they get their way, our future is hunger. We've seen what happens – people coming to the town and turning to crime. That's the future for our children if we don't stop it now. What they call progress means the end for us. When they've finished there'll be no rubber trees, no Brazil nut trees, not even their cattle – just dust."*

"What they call progress means the end for us."

The state government of Acre claims that Brazilian rubber is not economically viable – that it would be cheaper for Brazil to import Malaysian rubber, and that the domestic use of Acre's rubber is effectively a subsidy to the rubber-tappers. The rubber-tappers hotly deny this. They put the problems of the Brazilian rubber industry down to the lack of investment. Poor transport facilities, for example, mean many lost days of production transporting rubber and Brazil nuts to market. In the municipality of Feijó, for example, Juarez Leitão dos Santos of the Rural Workers' Union calculated that it costs 100 days to transport 10,000 kilos to market – 20 men each transporting 500 kilos and travelling for five days. Similar journeys are necessary to seek medical care when someone is sick or injured. On top of lost production time, the cost of transporting each kilo of rubber is high when such small quantities are involved. Juarez dreams of a network of cooperatives and clinics in the forest, as well as fuller exploitation of other forest products. With this kind of investment, he asserts, the costs of production would drop dramatically.

In July 1988, following a series of *empates* (peaceful attempts to occupy disputed sites) that were met with violence, the rubber-tappers' pressure and that of their international allies met with their first success: the state government of Acre ordered the expropriation of the 6,000-hectare Cachoeira rubber estate and

Chico Mendes (right) with the mother of a rubber-tapper reputedly shot dead by a landowner's hired gunman; Chico himself was murdered soon afterwards on the orders of the same landowner. (Neil MacDonald/ Oxfam)

its handover to the rubber-tappers to form the first-ever extractive reserve. This victory precipitated Chico's assassination. Cachoeira had belonged to the landowner Darli da Silva, who reputedly swore to 'get' Chico. On 22 December 1988 he was gunned down in the doorway of his house, leaving behind a young widow and a child. International outcry was almost instantaneous. Trade union and political figures flew from all over Brazil to the funeral in Rio Branco on Christmas Day. A reported 4,000 people accompanied the cortege. Darli and his son Darci were arrested, and at their trial in December 1990 were each sentenced to 19 years in prison, the father for ordering the murder, and the son for pulling the trigger.

Since Cachoeira, other extractive reserves have been mapped out, covering a million hectares. But the rubber-tappers' new leader, Julio Barbosa, says that this is a drop in the ocean, compared with the estates of a million hectares or more that a single rancher may hold. The rubber-tappers of the town of Feijó, for example, feel that all the international attention on Xapurí has brought them little. Juarez Leitão dos Santos described proposing projects to the National Council of Rubber-Tappers and getting no answer. *"This region has been abandoned"*, he said. *"Even by the National Council."* He felt that the National Council was remote, and never came to visit the rubber estates.

PROFIT, ECOLOGY AND PEOPLE

Brazilian governments have come under international pressure in recent years over environmental policies. International agencies, including Oxfam, have helped rubber-tappers, peasants and Indians to present their case to the international community. International environmental concern has helped to convince the World Bank to withdraw funding for big projects. But the importance of international support depends on understanding the real issues at stake.

Extractive Reserves designated or in progress

Name	*Area*	*State*	*Status*	*Population*
São Luis do Remanso	39,752 ha	Acre	Functioning	130 families
Santa Quitéria	44,000 ha	Acre	Functioning	150 families
Cachoeira	24,973 ha	Acre	Functioning	80 families
Macuauä	103,000 ha	Acre	Functioning	343 families
Maracá 1	75,000 ha	Amapá	Functioning	214 families
Maracá 2	22,500 ha	Amapá	Functioning	94 families
Maracá 3	226,500 ha	Amapá	Functioning	760 families
Antimari	260,227 ha	Amazonas	Functioning	867 families
Terruã	139,295 ha	Amazonas	Functioning	126 families
Polígno dos Castanhais	200,000 ha	Pará	Land obtained	200 families
Rio Ouro Preto	130,000 ha	Rondônia	50% land obtained	220 families
Rio Pacaas Novos	140,000 ha	Rondônia	part land obtained	110 families
Rio Cautário	145,000 ha	Rondônia	50% land obtained	150 families
Rio Pedras Negras	180,000 ha	Rondônia	50% land obtained	unknown
Rio Jaci/Mutum Paraná	192,000 ha	Rondônia	part land obtained	unknown
TOTAL	1,922,247 ha			3,244 families

(Source: Adapted from ***Tempo e presença****, pp. 244/245; 1989, CEDI, São Paulo)*

The rubber-tappers are worried by government plans to create 'national forests'. One national forest of 450,000 hectares has already been decreed. They see this as responding to international concern for the Amazon rainforest without taking forest-dwellers into account. Gatão, a member of the National Council of Rubber-Tappers, commented: *"They created this idea and then went out to Europe and the US with it. They will take the people out of the forest, leaving it clean, tidy, with the big companies in charge."* By contrast, their own demand for extractive reserves puts the forest-dwellers themselves and the Indians at the centre of the proposal. Ceu do Mapia, a so-called 'extractive reserve' created in 1989, is the embodiment of the rubber-tappers' fears. Two authors of a recent study of the rainforest observe:

> *"... as tappers and Indians pressed for further extractive reserves, the Brazilian press trumpeted the establishment of just such a reserve – Ceu do Mapia – on the border of Acre and Amazonas and hailed it as the elimination of all Chico Mendes' fondest dreams. Established in a national forest (and hence carrying no intimations*

of land reform) Ceu do Mapia turns out to be basically an agricultural colony for the devotees of the cult of the Santo Daime. Established in the 1970s, the cult focuses on the spiritual use of ayahuasca, the psychedelic vine...

Approved with lightning speed by President Sarney, Ceu do Mapia stood in marked contrast to other reserves where arduous processes of expropriation have stretched into years. While the total budget for the two existing reserves was less than £130,000, Ceu do Mapia's hydroplane, ice factories and working capital added up to a budget of £4.5 million.

Co-opting the language of environmentalists and the idea of extractive reserves, the project has no political content, implies no change in existing conditions of land tenure or justice and is mainly a site for prosperous young refugees from the life of the Brazilian elite."[7]

The 'Ecological Reserve' built by the Albras Aluminium Refinery in the state of Pará is another example of the problem. It is described by the company as an ecological showpiece. But it has nothing to do with people.

On the road to the refinery there are billboards placed at intervals saying "Explain to your friend the importance of the environment". They have put an enormous area of the forest behind barbed wire. This is the 'ecological reserve' – an area to be preserved as virgin forest. To ensure that it remains virgin, it is patrolled by 'ecological guards' to keep the people out. Here and there, on Albras/Alunorte's land you can see the semicircles of fruit trees that are all that indicate where a home once stood. The reserve was created by the simple expedient of driving local people out.

Conde: the death of a community

Conde is a village in the shadow of the smelter. Before the smelter came, it was a little riverside village with a spectacular beach. The villagers lived simply: a little fishing, a little farming. But their land was appropriated by Albras/Alunorte, and the beach was dredged up and taken a mile downriver to construct a riverside dock. An Oxfam visitor wrote the following description of the changes the smelter has brought to Conde.

"Driving into the centre of the village was like entering a ghost town. Every other little wooden building was a bar. Most are closed now. The painting on their shutters has flaked. The gaudy signs are hanging awry. A few years ago the village catered to the 5,000 construction workers from the smelter. Conde became a wide-open town. Drunk workers brawled in the streets, blowing their wages on cachaça [raw cane alcohol] *and whores. The daughters of the fisherfolk became prostitutes, their fathers brothel-keepers for Albras/Alunorte. Now the glitter is gone. The few bars that are open are largely empty.*

The village is marking time, hoping for better days. It can never go back to what it was. A lone fishing canoe, slipping out between the palm trees on wine-red waters against the red disc of the dying sun, was the only vestige we saw of Conde's past life."

(Andrew Couldridge/Oxfam)

PART III: INDUSTRIALISATION

Introduction

"With all this increase in speed everywhere else, things here are slowing down."

(Fisherman, São Luis)

In the late 1970s the focus of new industrial growth shifted from the south to the Amazon north. This represented a new phase in the military government's plan to modernise Brazil. In the 1960s the generals' strategy had been to produce goods, mainly in southern factories, for the home market. By the mid-1970s they looked to export earnings as a way of fuelling development.

Between 1968 and 1974, the generals had produced the so-called 'economic miracle', during which the economy grew at around 10 per cent a year. Foreign companies were encouraged to invest heavily, mainly in the south, particularly in the motor industry (and ancillary industries such as tyres) and household electronic goods, as well as, to a lesser extent, in pharmaceuticals and plastics. At the same time, the state had concentrated on large infrastructural projects such as dams and roads.

Hydroelectric dam at Paulo Afonso Falls, Bahia.
(Andrew Couldridge/ Oxfam)

But then the 'miracle' ran out of steam in the mid-1970s, due to a combination of three reasons. Firstly, the international oil crisis led to vastly greater fuel import costs. Secondly, much of the money for the investment had been borrowed on the international market, and debt repayments started to snowball as hard currency interest rates rose. Thirdly, the 'miracle' stood on shaky social foundations. It had produced a new middle-class consumer market, while worsening the condition of the workers and peasants. In 1960, the poorest half of the population received 1.5 per cent of the national income; by 1972 this figure had fallen to 0.5 per cent. Brazil is the most polarised of all the countries in the world whose official statistics list income distribution. The military government's technocrats and the industrialists had borrowed to invest in economic growth, but had failed to produce development.

The planners were becoming aware of the commercial failure of most of the cattle-ranching projects. They began to pin their hopes on the exploitation of the newly-discovered mineral riches of Amazonia. Convinced that exports from the iron ore of Carajás, the gold of Serra Pelada and the bauxite of Trombetas would repay their investment, they continued to borrow heavily on international markets in an increasingly fevered rush to maintain growth and service the mounting debt. The pace of the 'big development' projects accelerated in the late 1970s, not only because of the external economic crisis, but also because of a growing domestic debt. 'Big development' became an unstoppable juggernaut.

THE DEBT TIME-BOMB

Social upheaval, violence and despoilation have been the social and ecological consequences of Brazil's headlong modernisation. The economic costs are evident in its international debt of US$112 billion – the largest absolute debt of any Third World country. How did this come about?

The international debt crisis is often explained by the oil price rise of 1974 by the OPEC countries. The oil price increase certainly had major economic effects world-wide: it slowed down economic activity, increased fuel import bills in non-oil-producing countries, and confronted international banks with the need to find ways of recycling petro-dollars. But the fuse of Brazil's debt time-bomb was lit before the oil crisis. Successive military governments after 1964 entertained the grandiose dream of turning Brazil into a world economic power. The years of the 'economic miracle' between 1969 and 1973 saw foreign debt grow by a (then) massive US$10bn.

Paradoxically, there was no need for this borrowing. Brazil's foreign trade was in balance, and US$6bn of the borrowed money remained unused – deposited abroad. There were two reasons. Firstly, with the economy growing at around 10 per cent a year, Brazil's banks found it difficult to generate sufficient funds to keep pace with the level of investment. Secondly, the majority of the borrowing (60 per cent) was done by multinationals, who preferred to finance investment in Brazil by foreign borrowing rather than by transfer of capital to their local subsidiaries, because this provided them with ways of getting their profits out of the country more easily. A further reason for the debt was government 'vanity': several giant projects were aimed not primarily at development, but at providing a showcase for the new modern Brazil. Among these are the Rio/Niteroi bridge, and the vainglorious conceit of Brasilia – a new plate-glass and concrete capital carved out of the jungle.

By 1974 when the OPEC crisis hit, Brazil was already a 'debt junkie'. It was having to borrow more and more just to pay off its existing debt. In 1973 over half of all new borrowing (58.4 per cent) went straight back to foreign bankers as

Brasilia, the national capital carved out of the jungle. (Jenny Matthews/ Oxfam)

debt servicing. The oil crisis pushed Brazil deeper into debt. Determined to avoid a recession, the government borrowed almost another US$16bn between 1974 and 1976. The state overtook private borrowers as the main source of the debt burden. Through the state-run energy and steel sectors, the government borrowed more and more, and got less and less benefit from it: by 1980 servicing of the old debt consumed 95 per cent of new borrowing.

The time-bomb was on the verge of exploding. Throughout the 1970s, as the debt burden grew heavier, Brazil tried to export its way out of trouble. A series of mini-devaluations boosted export earnings, but the economy exacted its revenge, with inflation running at 46 per cent in 1979 and rising to 100 per cent in 1980. This was a major cause of widespread labour unrest in 1978-1980. By the end of 1980, the government was forced to restructure the economy to maintain the country's credit-worthiness. A trade deficit of US$2.8bn was converted into a surplus of $1.2bn in 1981. But social services and the domestic market were hit hard. Unemployment rocketed. Gross Domestic Product per capita plummeted by 4 per cent. The 'economic miracle' was over, and the poor suddenly felt the effects of the underlying crisis which the 'miracle' had hidden.

The shock tactics of 1980 persuaded the international banks to continue lending to Brazil. Between 1979 and 1982, the country borrowed a further US$63.4bn, in an increasingly desperate attempt to stave off default on its debt. Of the $63.4bn in new borrowing, $60.9bn never reached Brazil: it went back to the banks as debt servicing. But this was simply buying time that was rapidly running out. In September 1982 the clock reached zero-hour. Brazil ran out of foreign reserves, a month after Mexico sent shock waves around the financial world by announcing that it could not pay its debt. The debt crisis had arrived.

The Brazilian government officially declared a moratorium on its debt in January 1983. Rapid negotiations with the International Monetary Fund (IMF) produced a rescue package the following month. The IMF package forced Brazil to generate a trade surplus of US$6bn. Exports were to be boosted and imports cut, with state expenditure slashed. Brazil's trade surplus reached US$6.5bn in 1983 and topped US$13bn in 1984. The bankers were happy, but the economy was distorted to achieve this. None of the other targets negotiated with the IMF in 1983 and in six successive agreements up to 1985 was met. Inflation topped 200 per cent by the end of 1984. The money supply increased, the government deficit grew. The economy went into recession between 1981 and 1983.

The poor paid the heaviest price. Unemployment and underemployment rose to affect about one third of the economically active population. Wages fell and prices rose. The value of the minimum wage fell. By 1987 a worker on the minimum wage had to spend more than a third of it to buy one litre of milk and two small rolls of bread a day. Health standards deteriorated. Poor children were hit hard, suffering malnutrition and slashed education budgets. Riots and protests followed.

As the crisis grew, and protests along with it, the military handed power back to a civilian government, headed by José Sarney, in March 1985. A year later, in February 1986, a team of young economists headed by Finance Minister Dilson Funaro unveiled a new response to the economic crisis – the 'Cruzado Plan'. They rejected the 'orthodox' recipes of the IMF, which call for cuts in state expenditure and for the private sector to take the lead in economic revival. Instead, they were influenced by 'heterodox' economic theories which were also in vogue in Argentina and Peru. Inflation was reduced to zero at a stroke by introducing a new currency, the *cruzado*. Price controls allowed demand to rise, and the economy expanded out of recession. The foreign trade surplus had allowed Brazil to service its debt, while the domestic economy started to grow at 8 per cent. Negotiating from a position of strength, Brazil got agreement from the bankers in 1986 to put off its debt repayments for a year.

But the Cruzado Plan did not work for long. Domestic demand started to compete with production for export, which threatened the trade surplus. Merchants played their part in the collapse of the plan by withholding goods from the market in an attempt to defeat the price controls. Competition for scarce goods set off another inflationary cycle. By the end of 1987 inflation was running at 365 per cent, wiping out all the gains in wages since 1985. By mid-1987 Finance Minister Funaro had lost his job, and Brazil was again following 'orthodox' remedies. Attempts by the Brazilian government to impose a moratorium on its debt servicing were met with a hard line by the bankers. Starved of credit, Brazil was forced to give in and end the moratorium.

In 1989 to stave off inflation the currency was replaced by the new *cruzado*. But this was a temporary measure and inflation started to rise again, reaching 4853.9 per cent by the time the new government of Fernando Collor took office in March 1990. Collor introduced a drastic anti-inflation package. An old-style wage-price freeze was coupled with the super-monetarist strategy of freezing for 18 months savings accounts of US$1,000 or more. The introduction yet again of a new currency – the new *cruzeiro* – promised zero inflation. But exceptions made to the terms of the plan in order to stave off a severe recession produced monthly inflation at 5 per cent even in the first month of the new currency.

The recession mounted throughout the rest of the year, producing a wave of bankruptcies, but the government failed to contain inflation, which grew to a monthly level of 13.1 per cent in September 1990, according to the University of São Paulo. Prices of basic staples continued to rise, and a squeeze on agricultural credit was forecast to reduce harvests in 1991. Government attempts in October 1990 to convert Brazil's debt into government bonds were rejected by creditors.

THE CITIES

6

"*Constructing democracy is related to the problem of constructing citizenship.*"

(Brasílio Antonio Guerra, a legal aid worker in Recife)

Brazil is becoming one of the handful of Third World countries that are referred to as *newly-industrialised*. Its industrialisation is proceeding much faster and with even greater suffering than the turmoil of the Industrial Revolution in Britain. In Britain too, modernising landowners drove rural people violently from the land in 'Highland clearances' and the 'enclosures'. In Britain too, the landless people flocked to the cities, where they were confined in squalid slums and laboured in what the poet William Blake called 'dark satanic mills'. In Britain, the process of urbanisation occurred over 150 years. But in Brazil, much of this upheaval has happened in the space of one generation. In 1945 seven out of every ten Brazilians lived in the countryside. Today seven out of every ten live in cities. Even in the Amazon, more than half of the region's 12 million people live in the cities, particularly Manaus and Belém.

In the Amazon, many would-be colonists are forced into the slums of the new towns, trying to find work where they can. Here they are still second-class citizens. Marabá is one such town that has mushroomed in the forest without planning or the installation of proper infrastructure. The municipality had a population of 24,000 people in 1970. Today there are 350,000, with 70,000-80,000 in the urban area alone. But the school and hospital facilities are still those of the 1970s, intended for a population 20 times smaller. After the colonists and settlers came the construction workers on the Tucuruí dam, many of whom settled in the area when the work was finished on the dam. More people poured in during the early 1980s, drawn by the magnets of the giant Carajás project and the associated Serra Pelada goldfield.

It was boom time but, as in the frontier days of the USA, for every one who made it, there were scores of losers. Whole communities in the path of the new roads and the railroads were turned upside down. Along with the easy money went violence, land grabs, saloons and prostitution.

Once in the sprawling slums, known as *favelas*, of the cities, poor people face a host of problems. They need to find a place to live. Because few of them are able to find steady work, they cannot afford to rent proper houses. Having escaped

Women in a slum district of Recife discuss children's immunisation with a health group leader (left, in black dress).
(C. Pearson/Oxfam)

from the land squeeze in the countryside, they find themselves all over again caught up in a search for urban land on which they can build their homes. Property developers and civic authorities are now their main obstacles. Every city has its quota of homeless people, who sleep rough on the streets, most tragically the street children. Even when people have a precarious toehold on slum housing, they are still vulnerable: overcrowding, malnutrition and lack of services put their health at risk. So they must then fight for access to sanitation, health care and other services. Among those services is the right to public safety. Second-class citizens in so many other respects, their security needs are also often ignored by the police. Many slums are violent places where vigilante justice holds people in terror. This chapter looks at some examples of how slum-dwellers have faced up to these problems in the city of Recife, capital of the north-eastern state of Pernambuco, and in the town of Guarabira in the state of Paraiba.

URBAN LAND RIGHTS: ENTRE A PULSO

The Atlantic breakers roll up on to the sands of Boa Viagem, one of the most fashionable beach districts of Recife, the state capital of Pernambuco. High-rise apartment blocks line the seafront. But only a few blocks away is Entre a Pulso, a slum separated by a brick wall and barbed wire from the middle- and upper-classes of Boa Viagem. The high-rise apartments tower over Entre a Pulso like the battlements of a feudal keep. The landward border of the slum is formed by a new shopping complex which houses the Brazilian chain-store Lojas Americanas, as well as the Recife branches of international chains like C & A and Benetton.

Hemmed in by fences and walls, the people of Entre a Pulso are not part of the glitter beyond. The houses are small and cramped, some sleeping whole families in a single room. The most recent inhabitants still have earthen floors and crudely carpentered wooden walls. Some of the more durable concrete houses are ovens in the daytime sun. The narrow rutted streets are open sewers at all times, and rivers of mud during the rainy season. The people of Entre a Pulso are not considered clean and tidy enough to get jobs in the shopping centre, whose customers drive bumper to bumper through the *favela*.

Most of the slum-dwellers work irregularly as street sellers or odd-job people. Those nearest the shopping centre have set up businesses catering to the centre's workers – bars and lunch places.

Maria José Ferreira is 43. She moved to the city from the countryside in 1984, hoping for a better life. She has been one of the lucky ones. She works as a seamstress from her front room, making new clothes as well as mending old ones. She is fortunate to have this income. Her husband, who worked as a caretaker for one of Boa Viagem's apartment blocks, has lost his job. A big-hearted woman, she looks after six children – four of her own and two adopted. Between her dress-making, the housework and caring for the children, she puts in a 14-hour day, rising at 4.00 in the morning and finishing with supper at 6.00 in the evening. She sees many problems of life in the slum:

> *"There are so many children who don't have anybody to look after them properly. They don't have beds or mosquito nets. There is bad nutrition. They get skin diseases and stomach problems. People can't afford to buy the right food – they may only have beans and a little bread. Then there is the problem with the heat of the houses. Especially the cement ones get very hot. My neighbour has a little baby. It gets so hot she has to leave the house during the day. But there's nowhere to go."*

Entre a Pulso has been there in one form or another for 50 years, but the construction of the shopping centre destroyed much of it. Names of slums can be a clue to their age – the older slums have names that describe their origins, like 'Forced Entry', while newer slums tend to be named after TV programmes or films. The newest bit of Entre a Pulso is called 'Planet of the Apes', because the movie was playing when the land was taken over.

In the recent past, local governments saw slums as urban cancers and tried to eradicate them. But zoning of Recife in 1983 recognised the existence of 27 of the city's 200 slums, giving them a greater measure of security and the promise of services. By 1990 a further 11 slums had been recognised. This now gives them the right to representation on Commissions of Urbanisation and Legalisation (COMULs), urban development commissions that can draw on government funding.

This is where Arruar (literally 'roadify') can help. This small team of architects, engineers and lawyers (with funding from Oxfam) helps slum-dwellers in Entre a Pulso and other slums to develop urban improvement plans and then to negotiate these with the local authorities. Today Arruar is working towards trying to obtain legal title for the land in the communities it serves. Without legal ownership of their land, people in the city, as in the countryside, are at the mercy of land speculators. Some speculators wait until people have established a community on a patch of land, clearing and improving it, and then move in to evict people, violently or legally.

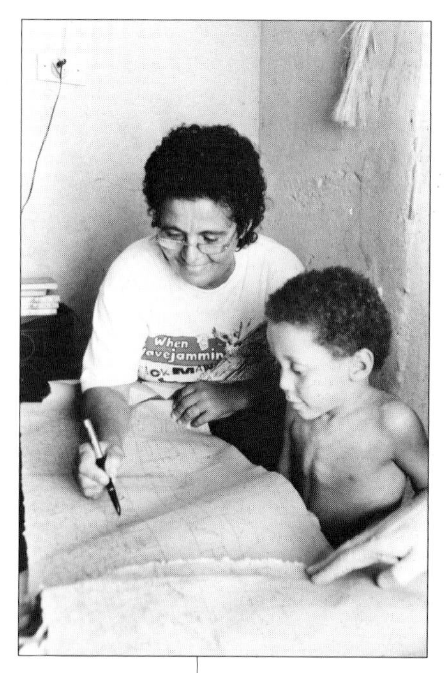

Maria José Ferreira, a seamstress in Entre a Pulso, draws a map of her neighbourhood for a slum improvement scheme. (Jenny Matthews/ Oxfam)

Football pitches are particularly vulnerable – large open spaces that attract the speculators. Space is at a premium everywhere in the slums, and only those best off have a small garden. A slightly enlarged turn of a corner becomes a municipal park. But in a football-mad country, the football pitch is a sacrosanct open space, respected by everyone within the community. Houses have been built right up to its limits, but no-one trespasses over that line.

Arruar have worked hard with the community to understand their use of space before submitting designs for urban improvement. Working with the community representatives, and before elaborating any plans, they ask residents to draw their own pictures of their environment, locating their house and the routes, buildings and spaces which are important to them. In Maria José's map, for example, the Community Centre is twice its correct proportionate size. As Milton, one of the architects, says, *"It's not our view which is important, but theirs."*

This way of involving people in analysing their own needs is coupled with joint decision-making. The community decides what development it wants, such as open space or community buildings like schools and creches. The architects draw up the plans, the engineers work on technical aspects such as drainage or structural considerations, and also analyse technical development plans coming from the local authority. The lawyer helps them fend off the developers.

Maria José says of the future: *"Sometimes I have no hope, but other times when I see that people are struggling to defend our right to stay here, I am hopeful. I have been in this community for six years. During those six years I have seen great improvements. People are making their houses better."*

HEALTH CARE: CASA AMARELA

Once communities have established their right to exist, they still need services, especially health care. Casa Amarela provides an example of what can be achieved. Located on the northern outskirts of Recife, it is the city's oldest slum. A vast and complex suburb, it is made up of many sub-districts and communities, ranging from shanty towns to longer-established low-income housing.

The hilly landscape complicates the standard problems of ill health and poor conditions of the wattle-and-daub tin-roofed houses. As well as the lack of water supplies and contamination of the narrow streets by waste, residents have to cope with the rivers of mud that cascade down the steep streets during the rainy season, sometimes dislodging homes.

Hunger, psychiatric problems, TB and parasitic diseases are common. High rates of child mortality are caused by respiratory infections, gastro-enteritis, dehydration and contagious diseases like polio, measles, chicken pox and diphtheria, against which children could be protected by simple immunisation.

Preventive health education, traditional remedies and community action can make a considerable difference. A health team (supported by Oxfam) working through a network of local 'health agents' is trying to work in all of these ways. All but one of the 50 health agents are women. They organise local health groups, and, here too, most members are women. Josilda de Araujo, the project coordinator, says that women, who are responsible for their families' health, respond better than men.

A health group

The people of one of the Casa Amarela neighbourhoods – Alto de José Bonifacio – won a bittersweet victory when the local authority opened a health post in December 1989 – with great fanfare (and with an eye on the local and national elections of October 1990). But the people are critical of the way it is functioning. A paediatrician, a clinician, a dentist and a nurse visit regularly. But they are not doing any preventive work. The people were insistent that they wanted not just any kind of health care, but for the health post to take on and support the work that the community is doing, emphasising prevention and education as well as cure. Maria Marta Delgado, a local health agent, said, *"We struggled for eight years for this health post. But we didn't want this kind of health post. You have to leave your house at one in the morning to queue up and get a ticket to be seen."*

The community group runs sessions which teach women about their own bodies. Using a cardboard model of a woman's body with detachable organs, they learn to locate the organs and discuss their function. This differs completely from the way the health post works, as Maria Marta explained: *"Here we have discussions with the women about cancer screening.* [Recife has a particularly high

Health education class in Casa Amarela, a poor district of Recife. (Jenny Matthews/ Oxfam)

level of cervical cancer.] *This service is not offered by the public health service. Or when it is, the women don't know what's happening – they're just thrown on to a slab and something's taken out or it isn't."*

The health post has started sending women to the group for screening. Maria Marta says: *"We don't want to be doing what the state should be doing. We just want to do this for a limited period of time and then move on to other areas. But they take the credit for this at the health post."*

Self-reliance and herbal medicine

The health project was started by Celerino Carriconde, a doctor who developed a particular interest in herbal medicine. Using traditional remedies is not only cheaper than industrial medicine, it gives people confidence in their own knowledge and culture – though enthusiasm can run ahead of proven medical benefit. A group of women works at the community pharmacy making the plants up into medicines, whose prices range from about 20 pence for camomile tea (a calmative) to 60 pence for a concoction of nuts, honey and several plants prescribed for sexual impotency. Maria Docarmo, the elderly pharmacist, insists that before use, any new treatment is discussed within the group and then with health agents and with other groups. They will test it first on themselves and their families.

They grow some 14 different species in the herb garden at the back. They use lemon grass, drunk as a tea, as a calmative. Marjoram is used as an infusion for earache, or, mixed with other plants in a bath, it is used to help aching bones. They say that comfrey has a multiplicity of uses – as a vaginal disinfectant, for gastritis (drunk as a tea), as an appetite stimulant (taken cold), as an appetite

A community health volunteer examines a patient in a herbal medicine clinic in Casa Amarela. (Jenny Matthews/ Oxfam)

depressant (taken hot), for anaemia (it has a high iron content), and as an antiseptic. Other plants are used for liver problems, for diarrhoea and many other complaints. Fatima, one of the project doctors, comments: *"This knowledge comes from the grandfathers and the great grandfathers. We technicians don't have this knowledge."*

From self-treatment to social services

Josilda, the project coordinator, gave examples of the campaigns they have run. Dirty water, contaminated with parasites, has been a problem in many communities. The first stage is for the health groups to discuss what can be done. So patients suffering gastro-intestinal infections will be treated with plants. But, as Josilda says, *"We can treat people, but the illness comes back again because of the conditions in which people have to live."*

So the long-term answer to health needs is to press the local authorities for sanitation. In most communities, as a result of citizens' action, the roads are now paved and the water is treated. The health agents are catalysts for their communities, not just for education in preventive medicine, but also to demand their rights from the local authorities. *"We move from health to social struggle"*, explained Josilda. The community health groups are linked both to the local residents' associations and to a national health movement – MOPS (the Popular Health Movement). *"The path to health"*, said Celerino, *"passes more through trade unions than it does through antibiotics."*

"The path to health passes more through trade unions than it does through antibiotics."

Maria Marta Delgado has learned this from her experience in health work. She is a health agent in the Alto de José Bonifacio neighbourhood. She is 22, single, and works in the hospital as a nursing assistant. Unlike most of the health agents, who have only primary education, Marta was educated to secondary level. She began to work for the benefit of her community when she was 18:

> *"I began to work with the residents' association and then I moved to health work. The struggle had begun many years before. It was for the basic things that we didn't have – electricity, water, a creche. We had hardly anything – no paving, no drains. Our struggle was for better living conditions.*
>
> *I only knew a few basic things when I started, a bit about plants. I needed some training. In FEACA (the Federation of Residents' Associations of Casa Amarela) there was a course each year, covering a variety of things – prevention, cure, first aid. The candidates are nominated by the assembly of the residents' association. They have to be people who have done work for the community. I was chosen from my community along with one other person. I had worked in the residents' association, typing up the bulletin.*
>
> *You can't separate health and mobilisation. Health is connected to everything else. There has to be mobilisation. People in Brazil don't have much education. Our work is one in which people can participate in anything we do. Curative work must be combined with education. To give people more strength and mobilise them for their rights. To have health you have to have a just salary. With that you can have decent housing conditions and decent food and nutrition, so you can avoid illness."*

SECURITY

Maria Marta and the people of Alto de José Bonifacio are proud of one of their recent gains: they successfully pressured for a police station in the neighbourhood. Many slum communities have no policing, and have become dangerous places in the grip of vigilante groups. Although Brazil's rural violence has started to make international headlines, the level of urban violence is higher. In São Paulo one street child a day is murdered. In the three years up to 1990 in the state of Pernambuco, 1,000 people have been killed, most of them in the metropolitan area. The people responsible are urban vigilantes – death squads.

Unlike the gunmen in the rural areas, these death squads are not political. Their victims are not leaders and activists in the popular movement, but drug traffickers, car thieves, petty criminals. The death squads say they are dealing with delinquency. This gives them some moral legitimacy in the communities: people support them because they are the only 'law' around. But they also create a climate of fear in the communities. The death squads are available for hire by shop-keepers, local tradesmen or by criminal gangs. Some squads have links to organised crime. There is evidence that some individual local and state police may be members, but no indication that this represents police policy. However, legal actions against the shadowy death squads have been few and far between.

The Recife-based human rights group GAJOP (which is partly funded by Oxfam) says that only 54 cases out of every 100 violent deaths each year are brought to court by the police; and, of these, only 13 each year result in a conviction. GAJOP is working to improve the quality of public security. GAJOP workers say that the transition from military rule is not enough to build democracy. The coordinator, Brasílio Antonio Guerra, argues that *"Constructing democracy is related to the problem of constructing citizenship."* This means equipping people with an understanding of their legal rights, particularly in the field of public security. As one associate of GAJOP put it: *"Our basic objective is to empower the community in relation to the police, and to change the relationship of the police to that community."*

They do training work with church groups, residents' associations, women's groups and so on. One example of their success came in 1989 in a slum area of Recife, where the community was dissatisfied with the local policeman, who was accused of being incompetent and violent. He was also thought to have been involved with a death squad. The people united to demand their right to protection. Pressure on the chief of police got the policeman transferred.

GAJOP also provides communities with legal representation in cases that raise these general issues. In another community, police shot dead a young boy who worked in the rag-and-bone trade, collecting rubbish like cardboard for resale. The community was indignant. GAJOP provided lawyers for them to bring a prosecution. They feel that it is important in such cases that the community participate in every step of the judicial process. This is not only to demystify the legal system, but also because GAJOP will follow such cases to their conclusion only when the community are willing to do so, because of the danger of prosecuting the police.

WORK

Finding regular work is another struggle for slum-dwellers. It is particularly hard for women, for whom domestic service is often one of the few kinds of work available. Domestic workers represent arguably the most exploited of Brazil's occupations. Brazilian law has only recently recognised domestic work as an occupation, and these women still do not enjoy the same constitutional rights as other workers. At least on paper, other workers are entitled to paid holidays, maternity leave, a 40-hour week, and employers' pension contributions. Domestics are struggling to be recognised as workers and win these rights. Oxfam supports domestic workers' unions in the states of Pernambuco, Paraiba and Bahia.

The Association of Washerwomen and Domestic Workers of Guarabira in Paraiba was founded on International Women's Day 1982. Members who work as maids can work as much as a 16-hour day for as little as US$6 a month. Maria Fatima de Lima do Nascimento, a washerwoman, is the president of the Association. She says:

> *"To be a maid is to be treated as an object. We get a little room in the employer's house; unpainted, with a bed. Often it's just in a little storeroom. They employ young girls from the country because they are more malleable. They give them money every now and again to visit their families; every two months maybe. They don't respect our rights. The constitution says we should get a minimum salary, and fixes the working day at eight hours – 40 hours a week. But they don't want to pay this. They say that because we eat and sleep in their houses and they give us old clothes, we are not entitled to a minimum salary. They say if we want a minimum salary, these things will have to be deducted. As for the girls who sleep in the houses: at night the husbands force them to have sex with them. Then when they get pregnant they throw them out and claim it was a lover."*

By 1990 the Association (which is supported by Oxfam) had 200 members. It meets every Sunday. But, since this is usually the only free day that many domestics get, attendance at meetings is low, and it is hard to recruit members. The Association runs training courses in cooking, nutrition and dress-making,to improve the women's chances of employment, and provides legal aid. A literacy class for children was not very success-ful. But they have succeeded in winning standardised minimum rates for washerwomen through drawing up a price list.

Maria Fatima de Lima do Nascimento, the president of the Association of Washerwomen and Domestic Workers of Guarabira, Paraiba state.
(Jenny Matthews/ Oxfam)

The legacy of the car workers

The domestics and washerwomen, like many poor people, have little power. But many groups in Brazil, from rural workers to slum-dwellers, have been inspired by a sector with much more clout: the car-workers of São Paulo. In 1978 a strike in that state proved that the poor could make their needs felt, and it signalled the beginning of the end for the military government. The wave of industrialisation during the 'miracle' had created a highly concentrated working class in the big cities of the south: in 1968 the biggest factories did not employ more than 5,000 workers; in 1978 there were 38,000 workers at Volkswagen alone and 25,000 at Ford. There were 210,000 metal workers in the 'ABC' industrial belt around São Paulo.

On 12 May 1978 a strike against the labour code of the military government broke out in the Saab-Scania plant. The strike spread rapidly throughout the motor industry in the ABC industrial belt to involve half a million workers at 400 factories in 18 towns in São Paulo state. Striking workers won concessions on job security and compensation for inflation. Luís Inácio da Silva (Lula), later to be a presidential candidate in 1989, emerged as a leader in these strikes. The strike wave also challenged the old leadership in the unions – the pro-government figures described as *pelegos* (sell-outs).

The previously hard-line military government was forced to adopt a more conciliatory stance when General Figueiredo became President in 1979, ushering in the policy known as *abertura* (opening). But the strikes continued: 185,000 metalworkers in ABC came out on strike on the day of Figueiredo's investiture, demanding a 78.1 per cent pay rise (with inflation running at 46 per cent). The strike was settled for 63 per cent. The strike wave spread, involving nurses, teachers, bank workers, doctors, and even military policemen. In November the government brought in new wage legislation which halted a number of the strikes – making six-monthly wage adjustments for inflation, and redistributing income from higher-paid to lower-paid workers. The following year, 1980, also saw the first strikes by rural workers, which were supported by the church. Today many poor Brazilians who are actively working for improvements in their communities describe 1978 as the moment when things began to change for them.

FROM PEASANTS TO WORKERS

7

In the late 1960s a helicopter owned by US Steel had to make an emergency landing in the southern Pará jungle. It landed on an exposed range of hills – the Serra dos Carajás. One of the passengers was a geologist. He instantly recognised why the hillside supported no vegetation: it was composed of high-grade iron ore. Today Carajás has become the biggest of Brazil's mega-development projects.

The iron deposits form the core of an integrated development area, including mining, logging, iron and aluminium smelting, and agro-industrial plantations. There, some 800,000 square kilometres of Amazonian forest (10 per cent of Brazil's national territory and bigger than the United Kingdom and France together) is being clearcut, bulldozed and mined. In the states of Maranhão and Pará, farming communities have had to watch in despair as their houses, crops, orchards and nut trees are bulldozed to make way for steel plants, fuel terminals, and property development. Pig-iron smelters are being established, paving the way for a steel belt that will rival the German Ruhr. The forest around is being felled for timber and charcoal. The cleared land is being planted with export crops like black pepper, oil palm, bananas and pineapples. Gold mines and aluminium smelters are mushrooming where once there were trees. Power lines stalk through the forest, carrying power from the giant Tucuruí dam to the new industries.

There are estimated to be 18 billion tonnes of iron ore in Carajás. The concession to the area is held by the state Companhia Vale do Rio Doce (CVRD), which established a joint venture with US Steel and then bought out its US partner. The zone is also estimated to contain rich deposits of other minerals: manganese, copper, bauxite, nickel, cassiterite and gold. The region is planned to generate $17bn a year in export earnings in the 1990s. Since Minas Gerais supplies all Brazil's domestic needs, all the Carajás production will go down the rail line to the São Luis terminal for export to Europe, North America, and Japan. In 1987 35m tonnes of iron ore were exported, and the target figure is 50m tonnes. They are talking now of doubling the rail line. Even at that rate of extraction, the Carajás ironfields are estimated to have 350-400 years' worth of reserves.

Iron-ore mining at Carajás.
(Anthony Hall/ Oxfam)

Six trains a day, of 200 wagons each, travel the new 900 km railroad from the Carajás mines to the CVRD terminal at São Luis. The rail-line, which forms the backbone of the programme, passes through and is transforming 131 municipalities. The iron ore dumped by the trains travels the last half mile by conveyor belt to a pipe hanging over the water. And the wealth torn out of the tormented earth of Carajás spews finally out of this pipe into the holds of waiting European ships. The European Community is the largest funder of the iron ore project. The European Iron and Steel Confederation put up a loan of US$600m, and European banks lent a further $450m. The World Bank contributed $300m. In return, the European Community has been guaranteed 13.6 million tons a year for 15 years, reportedly at 'banana' prices. This amounts to one-third of Carajás' production and half of the Community's total needs for iron ore imports.

Atop it all is the powerful CVRD company. In addition to the iron fields and the rail line, it owns half of the Alumar and Alnorte aluminium smelters.

For poor communities in the area, the development programme offers them only dispossession. Many now live, the children pot-bellied from starvation, in squatter camps by the roadsides. Violence has erupted over land disputes, as land grabs by the rich and powerful have forced hopes of land reform into the background. The area is in turmoil: thousands of landless peasants are on the move, looking for new ways of making a living, leaving behind a growing number of women-headed households; immigrants are streaming in from other parts of Brazil, hoping for a new future in the steel mills, the logging camps and, especially, the gold fields. As Amazonia becomes the new industrial centre of Brazil, whole communities and ways of life are being transformed. Peasants have no choice but to become industrial workers.

LOGGING IN PARAGOMINAS

One of the biggest new industries is timber. Commercial logging is the second largest cause of tropical deforestation in the world. Much of it is used for firewood or charcoal. The development of iron smelting in the Carajás project has dramatically enlarged the appetite for charcoal, which is used as a catalyst in the process. The export of tropical hardwood for construction in developed countries provides a major market. More than half of all the world's tropical hardwood exports go to Japan. Western Europe is the second largest customer.

Going for short-term profit is the policy of commercial companies. They have little incentive to replant the trees, in order to make logging a sustainable industry. Instead the companies simply move on, once they have finished exploiting an area of virgin forest – leaving behind devastated land and logging towns with no future. The forests have already been exploited in Espírito Santo in the south. Now Paragominas, carved out of the jungle 23 years ago in the Amazonian state of Pará, and one of the areas designated for 'development' in the Carajás project, has become the timber capital of Brazil.

Paragominas is like some medieval painter's vision of hell. Fires burn across the valley, sending a pall of smoke hovering above the town. Smouldering sawdust piles, saw-mill chimneys, smokestacks from diesel motors, the clay igloo-like ovens for charcoal burning: all these contribute their wreaths of choking smoke. Saw-mills shriek from every corner, each giant angry buzz-saw tended by a group of sweating men and women.

Trucks roll in, carrying four or five huge trunks from the forest, coming from as far away as 300 km. Other trucks roll out, with the sawn timber for Belém, Brasilia or São Paulo. Bulldozers clash their gears, pushing protesting piles of offcuts across the mud.

Logging truck, Rondônia.
(Tony Gross/Oxfam)

"We need to tell the world that Brazil is eating itself up."

The workers live in a part of town called *Trecho Seco* – Dry Patch – which is simply a deforested area without services or amenities. The smoke palls that form from burning charcoal and sawdust fall as sooty deposits on houses, getting into people's lungs. As the iron-smelting plants in the towns of Acailandia and Marabá come into operation, the local demand for charcoal will increase, leading to even more logging, deforestation and pollution. The flimsy company houses for the workers (from which they are ejected at a day's notice if they lose their jobs) are scattered like more detritus through the sea of mud. Everything is grey, brown or black-coated in soot from the ovens. The only touch of colour is the angry red of the fires, bright with the fever of the intense destruction. All the way around the horizon stands the denuded forest, the nearest trees blackened, bare and twisted skeletons.

There are 600 saw-mills in the municipality of Paragominas. One mill can saw up 500 trunks a day. This is the equivalent of 50 hectares (50 football pitches) of forest disappearing each day into the maw of Paragominas alone. João, a saw-mill worker, says: *"We need to tell the world that Brazil is eating itself up. We feel we're losing our health, which is obviously dear to us. But we're also losing nature. We have to stop this tree business. The Amazon is the lung of the world."*

Conditions in the saw-mills are appalling. Brazilian labour law is largely ignored. A male worker puts in a ten-and-a-half-hour day, from 6.30 in the morning to 6.30 at night with an hour-and-a-half for lunch. He works six days a week – making for a 63-hour-week, even though the 48-hour-week is theoretically a legal right. Feeding the trunks through the buzz-saw, he may earn £3.70 a week – considerably less than the statutory minimum wage. Safety provisions are minimal and are regarded as the workers' responsibility, as João can testify: *"The workers have to buy their own safety clothing. Gloves cost $1. Protective goggles are $4. The boss doesn't provide helmets. He said he couldn't afford them. In my workplace only three people out of 16 have signed workcards. If someone gets sick, they just have to look after themselves."*

The work is constant and hard. Two men together push the long vertical sections of trees through the saw-blade, a third man steadying it as it comes through. Children as young as 11 years old, pushing wheelbarrows full of sawdust and offcuts, toil between the mill and the ever-growing tips. People cough continually: living day and night on the edge of the mills, they are constantly sick. In João's words:

> *"It's difficult to avoid sickness, because of the constant pollution in the air. During the day because of the sawdust. During the night because of the smoke from the fires. Most people live right next to the mills. There's no getting away from it. The conditions are really bad. There's no water, no electricity, no toilets. A toilet is a hole in the ground with wood over it, and everyone uses it. The company provides housing. But if you get the sack you have to leave within 24 hours or the police come."*

But the feverish pace of destruction is already burning itself out. Already 20 per cent of the saw-mills have shut down. In a matter of a decade or two, Paragominas will be worked out as a timber town. A saw-mill owner confessed:

"The wood is running out. We bring trees now from as far away as 50 to 100 kilometres. Ten years ago we bought from closer in. There is some replanting with fast-growing trees. But the trees we use are never less than 30 years old. Some are up to 1,000 years maybe."

Saw-mill owner, Paragominas: "The trees we use are never less than 30 years old. Some are up to 1,000 years maybe."
(Frances Rubin/ Oxfam)

He recognised that protection for the environment was important, but claimed that he couldn't afford it. As far as he was concerned, that was the government's responsibility. He will move on. He has already moved once, from Espírito Santo when the wood ran out there.

When the money goes, it will leave the workers high and dry. Many, still rural workers in their minds, dream of a little plot of land. But in Pará, the ranching companies already have most of the land sewn up. David knows this to his cost. He is a veteran of four land takeovers, and was violently driven out of each one. He said, *"I'm finished now. I'm not in a state to struggle any more. I'm moving into buying trees and selling them."*

Now, with his wife, he manages a small sweet shop – a few plank walls knocked together in the dust of Paragominas, and very little on the shelves. His wife, amazingly enough in the grime and stench of Paragominas, is the local 'Avon lady'. She buys clothes and cosmetics from the representative who comes from Fortaleza, and sells them to her neighbours on an instalment plan.

David's main income, however, is from small-time logging. He makes few attempts to justify his new life as a small-time entrepreneur. It's not easy. He may have to go 70 kilometres for a tree. He may get only one tree a week. He buys a tree on the root from the squatters in the forest for £5.70. Though he sells it at the saw-mill gate for £57, he may make only between £2.85 and £4.25 profit after deducting his costs. He asks:

> *"What can you do? Poor people have to work any way they can. The jungle's disappearing slowly. Trees are big business here. The squatter is exploited. I'm exploited. The saw-mill owner gets all the profit. Our Brazil is rich, but it all goes into the hands of the rich."*

An old migrant from Bahia was perhaps more realistic than some of his colleagues when he recognised that, like it or not, he was now an industrial worker: *"We're in the saw-mills because we've got no option. If we try and work on the land, the gunmen will stick their guns down our throats."*

SINTICOMP

The old man from Bahia saw his future as lying with the trade union, which the workers have begun to establish – SINTICOMP. *"I like the idea of this union"*, he said, *"because we've seen some small improvements."* The union, whose education and networking programme is supported by Oxfam, has been able to make some small inroads into improving people's conditions. It was formed in 1984 with 150 members. By 1988 this had risen to 682, out of an estimated 18,000 workers. The union is still forced to lead a semi-clandestine existence, for fear of sackings or reprisals. The rank-and-file members dare not admit in their workplaces that they belong.

The union's main victory so far has been, ironically, success in winning workers' legal rights retrospectively in dismissal hearings. Sacked workers have won, through union representation, back-pay for overtime. The union fights unfair dismissals, such as the illegal dismissal of pregnant women. It is fighting for job security after a year's employment, for a reduction in hours to a defined working day at a guaranteed minimum salary with overtime paid for, and for safety equipment. In 1985 the union managed to stop most of the saw-mills in the city, and won a minimum wage with payment of unpaid backpay, and a reduction of hours.

Some members feel that the union is not doing enough, but it is arguable that unions, unfamiliar institutions for peasants dragged into the modern industrial world, are the best hope for developing plans for a more rational and sustainable use of natural resources, such as reafforestation. The workers, unlike the companies, have come to Paragominas to stay, and union officials like João are thinking about the future:

> *"All that's happening now is that all our wealth is being taken out and we're not getting anything for it. We and other families saw a way out in Pará because it's a super-rich state. But it's been an irrational exploitation of natural resources. If things were worked out better, Pará could be a refuge for all sorts of people, not just from Brazil. We ask everyone who can to help us. We have to put an end to this tree business. We need to have a campaign to alert people to the situation. The workers are accomplices to this situation. We have to get people to struggle for other things."*

Construction workers

The building of the Alunorte aluminium smelter at Vila do Conde, described in Chapter 5, created a boom in the region's construction industry. The smelter produces about 160,000 tons of aluminium a year, and exports much of it to the USA, Japan and Europe. A second phase is due to be completed in 1991 that will double its output. The plant is 51 per cent Brazilian-owned and 49 per cent foreign-owned (by Japanese and Canadian interests).

The Barcarena Construction Workers' Union organises 3,800 of the 8,000 workers in the sector, and is able to mobilise some 5,000 workers for its assemblies. Through a series of strikes that completely halted the construction of the smelter, it has been able to win agreement on minimum salaries, overtime, working conditions and safety. Barcarena construction workers have become the best paid in the state and the second-best paid in Brazil. However, despite this gain, the value of the salary has been gradually eroded. The minimum salary used to be 1.5 times the statutory minimum salary. Now it is on a par with the official minimum. Their strength, at first, took the companies by surprise. The union president, Antonio Ferreira de Silva, recalls: *"They thought we had nothing in our heads. They got a surprise. It wasn't even that most workers understood exactly what they were doing. It's just that conditions were so bad. The companies hadn't made any preparations. But, as we have got organised, so have they."*

Their work is harder now than it was in the early days of 1984/1985. Union activists face harassment. They are given the worst jobs, far away from the other workers. They are liable to be dismissed on any pretext. Antonio knows that he is on a blacklist, which he claims is enforced not by the construction companies but by the all-powerful Albras aluminium smelter. The employers have tried both the carrot and the stick:

> *"They try to co-opt you. They offer better salaries, better jobs. They've offered me various things. They offered to make me the head of a work team. They offered to transfer me to the office in Belém. All on condition that I gave up my post as president. When you don't accept things like this, they put on the pressure. They made me work in the rain without protective clothing. I've already been sacked once. I was out eight days, then I was readmitted with pressure from the workers – they threatened to go on strike. I know that to survive I have to keep at it. If they get me out, I won't get a job anywhere else."*

The union suffered a setback when a general strike in March 1989 provided the employers with an opportunity to get rid of several union leaders. Other workers were dismissed in the lay-offs that accompanied the cut-back in construction caused by the anti-inflation package of the new Collor government in April 1990. The union was able to secure redundancy payments, but it had to take the company to court to achieve them. A local advice and training centre, FASE, which is partly funded by Oxfam, provides support for the union and for agricultural workers in the region.

The agricultural workers, Mojú

Mojú, a river crossing near the city of Belém in Pará state, is designated under the Carajás plan for agro-industrial development. The Sococo company, which has 16,000 hectares, is part of the wave of agro-industrial companies, producing palm oil, coconuts and fruit juice, that moved into the area in the early 1980s. Sococo is planning to open a factory in Belém to process the coconut products.

Moises is a tough, street-wise operator. In 1988 he was a leading union activist on the Sococo plantation at Mojú. He is small and muscular, with the fine black hair and sharp features of his Indian ancestry. His brown eyes burned as he talked of his dismissal for trying to improve conditions on the plantation: *"We want to get back in so we can improve the conditions of work. It's like slavery."* His hard working life began in his childhood:

> *"You either survive or you die. I started work when I was 10 years old. I'm 23 now. I first started by selling coffee in Belém city. I did this for two years. Then I moved into fancy goods – selling jewellery and sunglasses in the street. Then I moved into fruit in the Ver-O-Peso market. Then I got into farmwork, clearing areas for people. After that I worked in the building industry in Belém. By this time I was 14. Next, I started cutting timber for charcoal making."*

A series of casual jobs in the construction industry, and odd jobs washing buses and doing car repairs, finally led him to work on the Sococo plantation:

Agricultural labourer, Paraiba state. (Jenny Matthews/ Oxfam)

> *"I make about £1.30 a day net. I work six days a week. There are about 750 workers and, over them, six or seven technicians. I've been working here for six months. My job is to weed the young coconut trees. Sococo also plants passion fruit, lemons and pumpkins. We only have a clocking-on time. No finishing time. The company decides how much work is to be done. The minimum amount of work is 60 trees. If you don't finish your quota, you get no pay.*
>
> *We get no meal at lunchtime. Then there's housing. Lots of people live far from the plantation. So they have to sleep in the fields. All they get is a shelter made with a tarpaulin. There have been problems of robbery and assaults. Everyone needs their own space. People complain a lot too about transport. Men and women are transported to the fields together. That creates problems. They just put 60 or 70 people in open dump trucks. Last year one turned over with 40 people in it. Thirty-eight people got fired for complaining."*

Health and safety conditions are appalling. Moises is particularly concerned about the dangers of chemical pesticides:

> *"The pesticides are sprayed from a tractor with two hose pipes on either side. The people who work regularly with the pesticides feel exhausted all the time. They get intoxication and skin rashes. Everyone gets some of this sometimes, because they spray where we're working in the fields. Sometimes it comes on the wind, intoxicating us. The group who work regularly with pesticides are given milk to strengthen them. They are given masks, but they might as well not have them: they're just a piece of plastic over the nose and mouth. There are no goggles, or gloves or boots. We don't have a doctor. There is no sickness pay from the company. They give us nothing, nothing, nothing. If you get ill, without the help of your friends you could die."*

FASE, the union and Sococo

Moises and some of his co-workers began drawing up a list of grievances. This cost him his job. They tried to meet in secret with the local Rural Workers' Union (STR). But the company heard about it. The next week they were fired.

The Sococo dismissals marked a new chapter in the history of the STR at Mojú. It was the first time the union had represented the agricultural wage workers, who form a growing part of the labour force in the area. By mid-1988, about 10 per cent of Sococo workers had joined the union: 70 men and women including Moises. They called the first of a series of strikes on the plantations in the area, demanding better pay and conditions, improved protection from dangerous chemicals, and, most basically, security of tenure for union members.

The strike spread throughout the company. Sococo became the first company in the area to agree a labour code on wages, transport, housing and protective clothing. But after the strike was over, the company ignored the last three elements of the code and the workers again went on strike in September 1988, paralysing production for nine days. Their demands were met and the union itself was recognised. Membership climbed to 230. By 1990, however, after the wave of enthusiasm passed, membership had declined again to about 70 and union activists were facing reprisals.

The involvement of the union in this fight for the wage labourers' rights was largely due to the local branch of FASE, the Brazilian Federation of Organisations for Social and Educational Assistance, based at Abaetetuba. They had argued long and hard with the union.

A lesson in development

Oxfam has helped to pay the costs of the FASE team in the area since 1972. Over the years, the team has radically changed its strategy for development. Many Brazilian development groups have been rethinking their work along similar lines.

For most of the 1970s, the FASE team concentrated on supporting a small number of model communities, by providing services like health care and legal aid, and introducing new cash crops. People's incomes went up, and their health improved. But all the time, the problems of poor people throughout the region were getting worse, especially when the Greater Carajás development programme started to disrupt their lives.

In 1979 the team decided to drop its small-scale work, and concentrate on giving poor people in the region the chance to make their voices heard and to express their needs. The team spread out, and helped local farmers to form self-help schemes and representative institutions. New grassroots leaders sprang from these groups, and the team helped to train them, so that they could contribute to discussions about the future of the region.

In the 1980s the FASE team supported community leaders in their efforts to make unions more democratic. Over time these institutions, previously government stooges, have become representative tribunes for the farmers. The team now concentrates on education, and on establishing local union branches (there are 14 so far), and on helping women to find a role in them. As new workers' sectors have emerged in the Carajás zones, such as agricultural labourers and construction workers, the FASE team has similarly advised them on developing democratic ways of working.

For several years the union had insisted that it existed to represent the small farmers only. The union felt it had enough on its hands dealing with violent land conflicts. On the road between Mojú and the Sococo plantation there is a roadside shrine to Virgilio Sacramento, president of the STR, who was killed in April 1987. Officially it was a road accident. He was crushed by a timber lorry while riding his motor bike. But the union think it was murder. Active union members have been threatened and ambushed by gunmen. Daniel, a union member, described how he had been dismissed for getting involved in 'too much agitation work'. *"If you work for progress"*, he said, *"they finish you. They just want to massacre you."*

The FASE team, part-funded by Oxfam, eventually convinced the union to broaden their activities. They felt that the wage labourers were the priority sector for the area, and through their mobility would bring valuable union experience to the more sedentary farmers. There are pros and cons. Though they may bring union experience and strengthen the leadership, there is a danger that the union becomes purely an instrument of their interests. Furthermore, they are a highly mobile group, as Moises' life history makes clear, and they may move on, destroying the continuity of leadership.

THE FISHING COMMUNITY OF JACAMIN

The Carajás development programme threatens some communities with the extinction of their way of life. The fisherpeople of the city of São Luis in the state of Maranhão face this threat. Eighty thousand people in the state make their living from subsistence fishing. Beyond the present limits of the industrial zone of São Luis, the way of life of the fisherpeople seems timeless and unchanged. But in a few short years, decades at most, the river banks will be lined with iron and aluminium smelters.

For now, however, forest and mangrove swamp accompany the wide sluggish river. There are a few nets stretched on poles in the water, and the occasional thatched hut, used as temporary dwellings by the fisherpeople working far from home.

Jacamin, on an island in the river, is home to one fishing community. The dispersed community of wattle-and-daub thatched houses with 800-1,000 residents lies up a narrow trail through the forest above the mangrove swamp and the exposed river silt that plops and sucks at the dank luxuriant bank. Fisherfolk scrambling ashore adopt a rapid rolling gait which skates them through the silt without touching the bottom.

Raimundo Ferreira lives alone. His small bare house is furnished only with a hammock, a table and wooden stools. His main livelihood comes from fishing, especially shrimp fishing. The community of 100 families also has plantations of maize, manioc, beans, rice, bananas and mangoes. He provides a picture of their way of life:

> *"The fisherman obeys the hours of the tide. So there is no night and no day. We could start work in the middle of the night or in the middle of the day. You just take advantage of the tide. For shrimps, you spend the whole time up to your neck in*

(C. Pearson/Oxfam)

water, two of you. With other types of fish, such as reje fish, you tie a net between poles fixed in the mud. When the tide rises the net rises, and you dive down and pull up the net. When the tide goes down again, you can collect the fish. You work together; groups of four, five or six, depending on the kind of net. We might work, I guess, about 12 hours a day. This is the work of the men. The women take care of the plantations. The men work in the fields too, but less. Normally, women do the weeding and the care of the land, while men do the clearing, planting and harvesting. A few women fish – inshore, with small nets."

In fact, women make a very significant economic contribution, catching molluscs and crustaceans in the inshore areas. Although some people have boats and some work in the boats of others, there is a lot of mutual help, and a fairly egalitarian distribution of the proceeds in this system:

> *"We look after the land together, helping each other out. We call this* mutirão. *We fish in order to sell. The principal fish is shrimp. We prepare the shrimp as well, drying it, cooking it and salting it. We have to do this because we don't have any ice. Many people don't have canoes. For four fishermen, and one boat, we divide the catch into five parts – one for the boat* [i.e. two shares for the boat owner]."

The underside of this subsistence lifestyle is lack of services. Though there is a school in the community, there is no doctor. The sick must walk two hours to the other side of the island, then travel one hour by canoe to the mainland, where they can either catch a bus into town or phone an ambulance. This is a community to which properly managed development could offer a lot. But though São Luis is growing explosively, the poor are marginalised. The old people remember the days when there were many more boats passing and stopping at the communities. Now, with fewer boats, Raimundo says: *"I can't understand this. With all this increase in speed everywhere else, things here are slowing down."*

The São Luis fisherfolk's main experience of Brazil's development is one of a threat to their livelihood. Rocketing property values have meant that weekend homes have displaced fishing families from the beaches. New industries and pesticides from ranches have polluted rivers, estuaries and lakes, while free-range cattle have stirred up the waters and disturbed fish-breeding cycles. Industrial fishing fleets threaten their livelihoods: a giant export terminal is being constructed and international deep-sea fishing is attracting many young fisherfolk, who are becoming wage labourers rather than self-employed fishers.

The people of Jacamin are only just up-river from the giant Alumar aluminium smelter, which is owned jointly by the Brazilian CVRD company, the Canadian company Alcoa, and Billiton (a local subsidiary of Shell). The construction of the smelter has already displaced 20,000 fisherfolk, and Alumar is expanding, threatening other communities. Alumar dredgers ply the river, keeping a channel open for the deep-water container ships. They dump their silt in the mouths of the inlets where the fishermen fish, blocking many completely and, by changing the topography of the river bed, altering the currents and the pattern of fish movement. In 1988 Raimundo and other fishermen estimated that fish catches, at some 200 kilos a week, were no more than half what they had been in 1986. Pollution, as well as the dredging, may have contributed to the declining catch. In 1987 a Korean oil tanker went aground, polluting the river and killing fish. Many people in the community also suffer from an itching skin complaint that they fear may be caused by pollution from the refinery.

Although they produce many of the things they need, they must also earn cash to pay for the nylon (for making nets), salt, sugar, kerosene and other goods that they cannot make. It is difficult for them to gauge, but they reckon that a single fisher may need to sell 100 kilos of fish a week to survive. So, declining fish catches clearly spell disaster. Worsening terms of trade add a further economic squeeze. In a six-month period in 1988 they saw the price of nylon double and the price of shrimp halve.

Raimundo and his friends are agreed that if they are to confront their problems, they need a stronger community voice and to unite with other fisherpeople around São Luis. They are members of the São Luis Colonia Z10, the equivalent of a trade union. But only 45 people in the community are members. Many people distrust it. The Colonias were set up by the military during the war to act as a naval reserve, and many remember this one's past oppressive history, which included arbitrarily denying people the right to fish. Raimundo is the local representative of the Colonia. He said: *"The Colonia is a support for the fisherpeople. Through the Colonia we have a means of knowing what our rights are."*

The Colonia has plans to improve the return to the fisherpeople from their catch by applying for a licence to sell directly to the consumers, cutting out the long chain of middlemen. The fish that they catch sells for over twice what they get for it. The Colonia also hopes to cut transportation costs by building more boats. However, they have only very vague ideas about the future.

The Catholic Church's Pastoral Commission for Fisherfolk (CPP) (funded by Oxfam) helps to strengthen the Colonia. Traditionally, the Colonias have been controlled by government or military figures. With the CPP's help, local leaders like Raimundo have won election to many of the colonias around São Luis, and turned them into representative institutions. This gives fisherpeople a chance to understand and affect the processes which are rapidly changing their way of life.

The CPP is conscious that the work is painfully slow and there is little time left. In 20 years' time, it is planned that the whole São Luis development area will be chock-a-block with aluminium smelters, steel works, container ports and commercial fishing terminals. They will pack, crush and ship out the wealth flowing from Carajás, and the wealth of the river and sea themselves. It is hard to picture these fisherfolk surviving the onslaught. Already they seem overwhelmed by the problems of declining catches, worsening terms of trade, and land grabs. But, even here, the experience of participating in a modern representative institution has taught them skills that will help them come to grips with whatever changes their lives undergo.

Celebrating National Fishermen's Day on an island near São Luis.
(Frances Rubin/Oxfam)

Goldmining at Serra Pelada, near Marabá. (Isabelle Butchinsky/ Oxfam)

GRASSROOTS CHALLENGES

8

Marabá is on the edge of the Carajás mining area, situated directly on the rail-line from the mines to the port at São Luis. A sprawling amalgam of three cities, it is another of the areas designed for 'development' in the Carajás plan. A few years ago Marabá was little more than a feudal village of Brazil-nut collectors, where a handful of aristocratic families held sway. The opening up of the Amazon displaced the old aristocrats, replacing them by new-style capitalists. Now Marabá is a boom town swelled by settlers, construction workers, and gold miners.

The Carajás enclave contains not only iron but also gold. The lure of instant wealth created a gold rush – an invasion of tens of thousands of poor men from all over Brazil, sweating, brawling and killing for the yellow metal. In 1983, at the height of the gold rush, there were 80,000 gold-panners (*garimpeiros*) working Serra Pelada near Marabá, the largest open-cast goldmine in the world. The mine is currently closed.

Serra Pelada is one massive hole in the ground. In full swing it looks like one of the monumental works of the ancient world. Men stripped to the waist, their bodies caked with mud, swarm up and down rickety wooden ladders. Continual lines carrying buckets of earth crawl their way up out of the pit, past descending lines returning to the earth. The competition of each against all, in which very few strike gold, leads to a brutal and violent life. Rampaging miners demanding better conditions have burnt banks and civic buildings in neighbouring towns.

When the rains start, the land itself becomes treacherous; many have lost their lives buried under mud-slides or plunging over the slippery precipices of Serra Pelada. In December 1987 miners demanding state support to improve safety conditions marched on Marabá. As they marched down the Carajás rail-line towards the town, police trapped them on a narrow bridge. The police advanced from both ends of the bridge, firing. An unknown number of miners were killed.

Uncontrolled goldmining has pitted the poor against the poor. Goldminers have invaded Indian lands, massacring whole communities, and Indians have hit back. Gold-panning in the rivers also damages the environment on which fisherpeople depend. The panners use mercury to extract the metal from its ores. The mercury poisons river life.

At the core of Marabá's modernisation is its 3,000-hectare industrial park, 15 kilometres outside town. Six iron smelters are planned here (to complement another 14 in a nearby town). The first, COSIPAR, opened in March 1988, with an output of 180 tonnes per day. Another 290 tonnes per day will be produced by the five other smelters. Total direct employment by 1991 is estimated to be 2,250 workers. Brazil plans to export one million tonnes a year of refined iron ore and pig iron, principally to Taiwan, China, South Korea, Japan, Germany and the USA. A steel works is planned once there are six to eight pig-iron smelters in production.

A year before the opening of COSIPAR, an Oxfam visitor gave this description of the industrial park.

> *"The area is virgin forest and the district when we visited it was simply a grid of future roads bulldozed through the forest. ... It is awesome I suppose to stand in a clearing in the middle of the forest and watch an iron smelter being set up, in the knowledge that this represents a first step in a plan to turn the whole Carajás corridor into a mineral working/heavy industry region that will rival the Ruhr and completely reorientate Brazil's industrial geography."*

The park is up-stream and up-wind of the town. So all the contaminated deposits from the industrial district will end up in the Itacaiunas river, and thus in Marabá's water supply. At the same time the prevailing wind during the day will carry pollution over the town. At night the wind dies down, so the pollution will settle in the town.

CEPASP is the Centre for Education, Research, Trade Union and Popular Advice. Founded in 1984, and funded partly by Oxfam, it is coordinating the resistance to the ecological and social damage inflicted by Marabá's growth. Environmental issues have become an urgent practical necessity for poor people, and for CEPASP educational and informational work around these issues is a priority.

Together with the local human rights group, they won a significant victory in a legal case with COSIPAR about pollution from the industrial park. The law requires each company to do an environmental-impact study, but COSIPAR failed to do this, saying that it would wait for a general study by the local Development Commission for Marabá. CEPASP obtained an injunction, based on a successful case brought by rubber-tappers in Acre, to force COSIPAR to do an environmental-impact study. In late 1990 the case was still stalled in Brasilia.

CEPASP has published its own audit of the impact of the industrial park.[8] It lists pollution by carbon monoxide, carbon, and methane, and the occurrence of acid rain and illnesses caused by the fumes. But it notes that the impact of the pig-iron industry goes far beyond urban pollution: another major concern of CEPASP is the problem of charcoal production. Charcoal is used as a reducing agent in the refining of iron. The industrial development of Marabá alone will consume almost one million tonnes of charcoal by 1991. This means the deforestation of 50,815 hectares of forest a year, and a loss of around 32,500

Charcoal burning, Acailandia, Maranhão. (Jenny Matthews/ Oxfam)

tonnes of soil nutrients. The soil will become impoverished and eroded, and the rivers blocked. Numerous plant and animal species will disappear. The production of charcoal in turn will have further social and economic effects: the Greater Carajás Project estimates that Marabá's industrialisation will generate 13,714 indirect jobs. But 85 per cent of them will be in charcoal burning, with potentially devastating results, as CEPASP's Raimundo Gomes da Cruz Neto explains:

> *"Deforestation is not the only disaster. There's also a disaster for the communities of small producers in the area. [Because there is no state agricultural policy] what situation are small farmers going to be left in? Because charcoal production is more profitable than traditional agriculture. If they don't have help, they will be reduced to being charcoal burners for industrial projects. They'll leave their plots and just become migrant workers, moving round burning charcoal on ranches. This could have an effect on the small-scale production of cereals, since they won't have time to plant. We've already got a problem with food here in the region: fruit and vegetables are mostly imported from the south. Rice and beans are going to become a problem too."*

Experts believe that the Marabá iron industry is profitable only if the forest is regarded as what economists call an 'externality' – meaning that the wood costs nothing. Eventually, as the area around Marabá becomes deforested, the cost of charcoal will rise, pushing the smelters into non-profitability. CEPASP is not alone in recognising the long-term economic effects of the industrialisation:

Maritta Koch-Weser of the World Bank was quoted in the newspaper *Jornal do Brasil* in March 1988 as saying: *"For the Brazilian government it would be much cheaper to compensate the three companies who have already set up in the region and halt this kind of project than to ... reafforest a region bigger than many countries."*[9]

CEPASP has been organising meetings with agricultural communities, with unions and with residents' associations to explain the facts. It is producing leaflets and tape-slide shows to spread this information, because Raimundo fears that *"Unless they know the facts, people are likely to be in favour of projects that look economically interesting in the short term, but are fundamentally disadvantageous to them."*

In the longer term, CEPASP believes that unless an alternative development policy is put in place, the results will be disastrous:

> *"The proposal [is] to get the state to make a commitment to the development of agriculture, with real help for small producers so they can stay on the land. This government does not support the productive sector – everything goes to the private sector. In the Carajás programme, apart from minerals export, there is a production corridor for agro-exports either side of the rail line. They want to turn the rural area in this region into a region of great agricultural companies, using the big pool of labour provided by the* posseiros *who are squatting on the land."*

THE ITAPARICA DAM

Perhaps the most dramatic achievement of poor people in Brazil, afflicted by 'Big Development', has been that of the rural workers of Itaparica who took on the state and the World Bank to achieve compensation when a dam flooded their lands and homes.

In the north-eastern state of Pernambuco, there is no indication of the vanished town of Petrolandia. There is nothing, not even an old road sign. Just the eerie sight of a few roads that vanish abruptly into a lake. The lake was formed by the Itaparica dam on the São Francisco river whose gates closed in March 1988. But here in Petrolandia ordinary rural workers stopped the juggernaut of big development and won a major victory. Their direct protest and their international lobbying (which went as far as threatening a World Bank loan to Brazil) forced CHESF (the Hydroelectric Company of the São Francisco) to resettle them on new land, with salaries until they were able to re-establish farming. Marluce, one of the activists, was in no doubt of the scale of their victory:

> *"I don't know of any other country in the world where homeless people have got houses, landless people have got land, and people without work have got salaries. But it's not a total victory until the land is given over. If we stop here we don't go forward. Many people are going to get something who don't know how to use it, because they have worked all their lives for someone else. Most of the workers here don't realise that the wealth is created by their own efforts. They think it's created by the land-owners. Even though they know that the factory-owner never lifts a screwdriver and the land-owner never picks up a mattock, they think that it's those*

people who create the wealth. CHESF's propaganda is still strong. There are people who think that CHESF is a good company and just gave them houses out of the goodness of its heart, and they don't understand the pressure the union has put on over the years."

Agrovila 6, one of 102 resettlements, has a dreary regimented look with its grid of dirt streets lined by identical small whitewashed houses. But 66-year-old Agimir Tiburcio Torres, a silver-haired former share-cropper, is happy. His new house is better than he had before. After only six months he had produced a thriving garden. He proudly exhibited a watermelon from his garden, brandishing it high above his head like the winner of a sporting trophy. *"I feel like someone who's sold out to a politician just before an election"*, he cackled.

Agimir Tiburcio Torres with produce from his garden in Agrovila 6, a settlement for people displaced by the Itaparica Dam. (John Magrath/ Oxfam)

The campaign

In the early 1970s, plans for the construction of the dam first became public. The land of about two-thirds of the 120,000 farmers living and working around Petrolandia was threatened by the reservoir, planned to cover 834 square kilometres. There was already the experience up-river of the construction of Sobradinho, Latin America's biggest dam, where 72,000 people had lost their homes without compensation. As Marluce knew, *"There are people from Sobradinho begging under bridges in the cities."*

The Centre for the Defence of Human Rights (CDDH) (partly funded by Oxfam) was working to bring together farmers, church and union organisations to coordinate a campaign. It took around six years, until 1980, simply to get from CHESF an initial map of the area that would be flooded. Then they began their campaign for compensation.

At first, people could not comprehend the scale of the Itaparica project, let alone believe that their homes would be flooded. The campaign organisers helped them to understand, by taking people living close to the construction site to talk to people in more outlying areas. The campaigners urged that people should not allow themselves to be played off against each other by dealing with CHESF individually. Instead everyone was encouraged to work through the rural workers' movement. The *Polo Sindical* was formed as an alliance of all the rural workers' unions to carry out the campaign. The campaign also warned that people should not accept cash payments, which would rapidly become worthless because of Brazil's high inflation rate. They said the only adequate compensation was land-for-land, and demanded that the company buy land for resettlement.

By 1982, the campaign had broadened to five demands: land for those who were to lose theirs; houses for them to live in; basic amenities such as schools, health posts and drainage for the new communities; fair compensation for other property and assets (fruit trees, for example); and publication of a full map of the land to be affected. It took them until 1983 to get a complete map.

CHESF still refused to negotiate. The first direct actions took place in 1983: 'lie-ins' in front of the bulldozers at the dam site. In October 1985, construction was temporarily brought to a halt when 5,000 people took over the dam.

In 1986 the campaign moved into the international arena. The Brazilian government was trying to negotiate an Electrical Power section loan from the World Bank to complete this and other projects. One of the World Bank conditions for granting this type of loan was that people who were affected by the construction should be resettled. A number of agencies, including Oxfam, pointed out to the Bank that this condition was not being met in Itaparica. Oxfam was also able to talk this over with the UK government's Overseas Development Administration.

In November 1986 there was a week-long mass occupation of the dam site by 800 people. Agimir was one of the people who had occupied the dam site, despite the police guns and the threat of violence: *"I'm an old man, and it didn't seem to matter. I went out that morning not knowing if I was going to come back."*

Marluce was there too. *"It brought together people who had nothing left to lose and people who stood to lose everything"*, she says. Whole families took part, and especially women. When police reinforcements arrived, drew their batons and looked as if they would charge the crowd, the women took the initiative in trying to avoid conflict. They went to the front and linked arms because, in Marluce's words: *"We were afraid that if the men were at the front and they were hit by the police, they would hit back. And we didn't want that."* They started singing.

"Without land, without houses
Without anything to eat
What are the people of Sobradinho doing now?
What about us who still have houses and land
And stand to lose them?
What are we going to do about it?"

Later, at a point when they again thought the police were going to attack them, people began praying, and an old man started to recite the prayer of Our Lady (a traditional north-eastern prayer). The police didn't know what to do. Some took off their hats. Others crossed themselves. There was no violence. The occupation, Marluce says, was an act of desperation. But it paid off.

The rural workers' action and the international representations convinced the World Bank. The Bank informed CHESF that it would withhold final payment of the loan until the resettlement issue was resolved. CHESF finally agreed to build the agrovilas, with houses and land for each family, and payment of a salary until the first harvest or until six months after the project was fully functioning, whichever was sooner.

Victory

Marluce lives in Block 2, Agrovila 8 with her husband Januario and children in a three-bedroom house, with piped water and electricity. At night the lights of other agrovilas shimmer across the dry plain on the horizon and the sky is huge with stars. Asked how he liked having electricity for the first time, Januario looked into the house where his children were watching television and then looked at the sky before he answered: *"It's good. But the problem is that with electricity comes television, and with television you no longer look at the stars and the moon."*

People from Petrolandia were promised new housing in the new town of Novo Petrolandia. Rural people were promised new housing in 102 agrovilas on the Pernambuco side of the lake and seven on the Bahia side of the lake. The size of the houses people got depended on the size of house they had before. In the agrovilas, each was promised between 13 and 25 hectares of land, with between 3 and 6 hectares irrigated, depending on family size. Each agrovila was to have its own primary school, and secondary schools were to serve groups of neighbouring agrovilas. Each family was promised two-and-a-half-times the statutory minimum salary.

The unions say that 60 per cent of people are better off and 40 per cent worse off than before, but they say that even those who are worse off would have got nothing at all without the campaign. A few minutes outside Novo Petrolandia is a scattering of tents, huts and brick houses on the dry, stony earth. These are the people who had not believed that the union could do anything for them and took cash compensation from CHESF early on, in rapidly devaluing currency.

Problems

Belatedly, the World Bank and CHESF declare the resettlement to have been a success. However, many problems remain. Most importantly, in 1990, two years after the dam gates closed and people were resettled, they still did not have their land assigned. It had not yet been demarcated or irrigated. The Brazilian government pleaded lack of money. Though the World Bank approved a supplementary loan of US$100 million to complete the project, by late 1990 it had still not been paid out, because the Brazilian government had not put up its counterpart funding.

Natalicio Leite da Silva, father of 10, lives at Agrovila 6, block 2. For him, *"There is nothing to do except wander around in the bush. If you believe in what we are doing, the future will be better than what we had before. Right now it is worse."*

People arrived in the agrovilas between December 1987 and April 1988, expecting that the land would be cleared and ready for them to plant. In some

"It's hard to study when you're hungry."

cases they cleared the land themselves, in return for pay from CHESF, which reduced the boredom a little. But, in the confusion, there were cases of people clearing land that was not allocated to them. There have also been cases of old proprietors returning and reclaiming land allocated to the resettlement, because they say CHESF has not paid them. A particularly serious land dispute blew up at the end of 1989 with Pankararú Indians claiming the right to land that had been allocated to 400 families. Both sides are keen to settle the dispute by negotiation.

Without land to farm, people depend on the CHESF salaries. Leaders are worried about the psychological impact of these handouts. And there are economic problems. The salary is enough for young couples or single people, but is not enough to keep a family on. On top of this, in some places salaries do not get paid on time. The problems of living on these salaries have grown as the time without land has lengthened. In the words of one man in Agrovila 43 'PG': *"We had no money before, but we never went hungry. The salary is not enough to buy meat. To get meat before, we just went into the bush hunting, or killed one of our chickens."*

In the resettlement, women suffered a special discrimination. Though CHESF agreed that women contribute labour, the company assessed the value of one woman's labour, for the purpose of calculating compensation, as being worth half that of one man. The community argued that women worked harder than men and that this was not fair. CHESF agreed, but argued that women did not work in the fields as much as men, and they would not budge on this.

Many people are incensed too about the poor construction of their houses and the insanitary state of their water supplies. One resident of Brigida Agrovila 1 summed up their bitterness: *"We are not here to take out one harvest or to spend a six-months' holiday. We are here to live and raise families. But the construction company doesn't have the same attitude. The walls are cracking. The septic tanks aren't working properly."* The construction was done on the cheap, contracted out by CHESF. It took a lot of persuasion for CHESF to assume legal responsibility for the state of the houses.

People feel cheated by other unfulfilled promises of services, such as health posts, schools and transport. In Agrovila 15, a doctor visits for one four-hour day a week. He packs 35-40 consultations into a session, instead of the planned 20-22. As one resident put it: *"We don't consider that a consultation. The doctor tells you what's wrong with you before you even say anything."*

Fifteen-year-old Laura lives with her family in Agrovila 43 of the 'PG' group. Six months after they were resettled, the school had still not been built. Laura has to attend secondary school in the nearest town, Santa Maria, where she studies maths, Portuguese, geography, history, art, culture, science and religion. Her favourite subject is religion. She depends on public transport to get to Santa Maria, but the community lacks the feeder bus system it had hoped for. In order to get to school, Laura has to get up at 7.00 a.m. and walk to another agrovila to catch the 9.00 a.m. bus. The bus winds its way through six agrovilas and eventually hits the main road. There she waits for another bus, which gets her to Santa Maria for the start of school at 1.00 p.m. If the bus is on time, she might have half an hour to grab a bite to eat – a Coke and a pasty. If not, she goes

Homework for 15 year old Laura comes at the end of a 12-hour school day.
(John Magrath/ Oxfam)

straight into classes. *"It's hard to study when you're hungry"*, she says.

She gets the 6.15 p.m. bus back from town, arriving home between 8.30 and 9.30, depending on weather and road conditions. So, she will often have her first proper meal only at the end of this 12-hour day. When she gets home, she is usually too tired to do anything except sleep. Most of the weekend is spent doing homework. There is little time for games.

Most of the rural workers feel let down by CHESF. A man in Agrovila 1, Brigida, complained: *"We were wooed by CHESF's pretty words, and left the land before we should have. We should have stayed and improved our bargaining position: stopped and not let them flood the land until they had complied* [with the agreements]. *But we believed them."*

THE NEED FOR GRASSROOTS ALTERNATIVES

Zé Preá, president of the Itacuruba STR and one of the best-known of the rural workers' leaders who led the campaign at Itaparica, summed up the people's challenge to big development:

> *"We need energy too. We are not against development. But the way it is done in Brazil, it doesn't take people into account. If they had built the dam and had everything ready for people to work the land, it would have been OK."*

The rural workers won a victory at Itaparica. The CEPASP challenge to the COSIPAR iron smelter at Marabá may have won them some space. But most important perhaps for the future is the emerging confidence among poor people that they can and must have a say in the development plans that affect their future. They are beginning to take up the lead given by the rubber-tappers and the Alliance of Forest Peoples, with their proposals for alternative plans, described earlier in this book. These alternative plans are important not only because they are more democratic. They are fundamentally important because planning for development that will last and that will safeguard the environment must start with each locality and micro-environment.

Zé Préa, president of the Rural Workers' Union in Itacuruba, Pernambuco state. (John Magrath/ Oxfam)

(John Magrath/Oxfam)

"The white man is walking in the dark, blinded by the glitter of gold. That is why he doesn't see us."

(Davi Yanomami)

Brazil is divided into two worlds – not just rich and poor, but its own internal First World and Third World. The giant Carajás Project, with its huge iron fields, its dams and its container ports, coexists with the embattled rubber-tappers of Acre, the impoverished sugar workers of Paraiba, the people without clean water or jobs in the slums of Recife, and the original Brazilians, like the Yanomami, fighting a life-and-death struggle to preserve their way of life.

The two Brazils represent two visions of development. The first is the live-for-today model of turbulent capitalist development. The other vision is of a sustainable use of natural resources which finds room for distinct ways of life and cultures, providing for tomorrow as well as today. The hallmarks of the first vision are the loss each year of over 17,000 square miles of forest (an area bigger than Switzerland), the cattle ranches which leave only dust after 20 years, the social and environmental tithe exacted by export industries just to service a growing debt burden, and the brutal deprivation of the slums. The words of Davi Yanomami are an indictment of that vision: *"The white man is walking in the dark, blinded by the glitter of gold. That is why he doesn't see us."*

The past two decades in Brazil have been a test of the two approaches. The military government of 1964-1985 pegged its hopes on an ideology of development. Its mission was to modernise and develop the country. The result was the 'economic miracle' of the 1970s. The Indians and the rubber-tappers, the rural workers and the slum-dwellers, experienced only *"destruction, behind a mask called progress"*. They learned from their experience. The poor have made great changes in tactics during this period. The partners with whom Oxfam works in Brazil represent a vision in which development means hope for the poor, and for the environment.

WHAT DO THE POOR WANT?

The poor of Brazil are not romantics: they have no vision of Brazil as an untouched primeval Garden of Eden. They are saddened by people in the rich countries who see the Amazon and the Third World as an ecological theme park – an environment without people. This book has tried to show that without people, there is no guarantee for the environment: the sterile ecological reserve of the Albras aluminium smelter at Vila do Conde (described in Chapter 5) is an example of where the theme park leads. Ecological reserves and national forests have no protection against future inappropriate exploitation. We have seen (in Chapter 2) how the gold prospectors in Roraima were moved out of Yanomami Indians' land and into a national forest. The developmental and environmental agendas have to coincide. They are complementary, because social injustice is a prime cause of environmental degradation.

The most clearly worked out case of a sustainable alternative is that of the rubber-tappers' Extractive Reserves. Creating an extractive reserve does not mean slapping a preservation order on a bit of the forest as a museum piece. It is a living strategy for development. The poor of Brazil want development, but development that is *for*, rather than at the cost of, people and the environment on which they depend. As Chico Mendes said: *"The rubber-tappers aren't saying that nobody should lay a finger on the Amazon. No. We've got our own proposals for organising production."*

And the rubber-tappers want more investment in the forest, to increase the productivity of their way of life. Neither do the Indians simply want to be left alone: they want a Brazil which recognises itself as multi-ethnic and in which they have the right to control their own development and the evolution of their own culture. This outlook is shared by Zé Preá, who said of the Itaparica dam: *"We need energy too. We are not against development. But the way it is done in Brazil, it doesn't take people into account. If they had built the dam and had everything ready for people to work the land, it would have been OK."*

In other areas of Brazilian life, clear alternative strategies have yet to emerge. A growing number of rural workers in the years between the ending of military rule in 1985 and the drafting of the new constitution in 1988 began to see sweeping land reform as the answer to their needs. And, as the analysis presented in Chapter 5 showed, the redistribution of land to small subsistence farms would not result in a drop in productivity – on the contrary, small farms are much more productive per hectare than is land devoted to cattle ranches or the traditional export-oriented estates. However, to achieve this in the north-east, and relieve the pressure on the fragile soil of the Amazon frontier, will need more than political will – it will also need substantial investment. Centuries of sugar mono-cropping have turned much of the north-east into a virtual dust-bowl. Reafforestation, irrigation, and soil enrichment programmes will be necessary to reverse the environmental destruction of the past.

The timber workers of Paragominas (whose story is told in Chapter 7) are beginning to look for long-term alternatives to the irrational exploitation of the

(Frances Rubin/Oxfam)

forest and for solutions that will sustain their community. Reafforestation and controlled timber harvesting are evident possibilities. And, like the shanty-town dwellers of the older cities such as Recife, they are looking for a standard of living that is compatible with basic human dignity. As Brazil becomes a predominantly urban society, people who were yesterday's peasant farmers are beginning to look to alternatives that improve the quality of urban life, rather than to a return to the land. The quality of urban life too is a part of the environment audit.

The slum-dwellers, like the Brazilian generals of the 1960s, are developing a vision of a Brazil that is in keeping with the country's economic potential. But it is a vision of jobs, of safe working conditions and of adequate public services, not just of ever-increasing exports. As Brasílio of the human rights organisation GAJOP said in Chapter 6: *"Constructing democracy is related to the problem of constructing citizenship"*.

CONSTRUCTING DEMOCRACY

Constructing citizenship is a good term for what the groups representing the poor of Brazil have been doing since before the military regime ended. They found no blessings in the 'economic miracle' and its sequels. They lost their land in increasingly violent land conflicts; they were driven into the slums without even basic health, welfare and education services. Only by their own efforts, as active citizens, were they able to achieve some improvements. As Celerino, the doctor who began the health project in Recife's Casa Amarela slum district, observed from his experience (see chapter 6): *"The path to health passes more through trade unions than it does through antibiotics"*.

In the harshest years of military rule, the Catholic Church provided one of the few safe spaces in which people could come together and work out common solutions to their problems. The vast majority of today's citizen activists had their first experience of taking control of their lives through the Church's grassroots Christian communities in the 1960s and 1970s.

In the 1970s things began to change as more and more people, Indians, rubber-tappers, rural workers and industrial workers, began to assert their rights to full citizenship of Brazil and to a fair share of its wealth. The growth of political maturity has been rapid and striking. New institutions and political parties have been created. Throughout society, more and more people have begun to participate actively in the debate about the future. In 1985, when Tancredo Neves was named by the military as President to head the transition to civilian rule and democracy, he was greeted with widespread popular enthusiasm.[10] A mere four years later, democracy was no longer an abstract hope: the 1989 Presidential elections offered a distinct political choice, represented by Luis Inácio da Silva ('Lula') of the left-wing Workers' Party (PT) and Collor, the right-wing final victor.

In between the two dates came the drafting of the constitution in 1988. At this time people gained their first experience of the modern parliamentary lobbying process. Chapter 2 noted the extensive campaign conducted by Indian groups

Protest camp outside a government building in Recife, 1987: urban and rural workers' groups unite to demand the redistribution of land.
(Antonio Melcop/ Oxfam)

and nations. Other groups too were actively lobbying. Rural workers, for example, were pressing for land reform. Women's groups were lobbying for a full recognition of domestics as wage workers. But this opportunity was new, and the capital, Brasilia, was remote from the lives of most groups of poor people: special assistance was required. Popular alternatives need alternative research, the building of networks that reach across the world, and technical support in legal aid and in lobbying. This was provided by a range of voluntary bodies that prepared research on the constitutional process and on political and economic issues, and gave advice on how to lobby. This too is part of the process of constructing citizenship, and Oxfam has supported the activities of several of these large and sophisticated organisations. The Brazilian Institute for Economic and Social Analyses (IBASE), which maintains up-to-date research on parliamentary policy, has been a long-standing project partner. It played a key role as a think-tank for lobbying on land reform. Several pro-Indian groups, such as the Pro-Indian Commission (CPI), the Catholic Indian Mission (CIMI) and the Ecumenical Centre for Documentation and Information (CEDI), helped Indian groups to present their case. A consortium of groups – CEDI, IBASE and INESC – maintains research on the debt problem.

The growth of neighbourhood committees, of Indian organisations, of the trade union movement and its national expressions like the CUT (United Workers' Centre), of political parties like the PT: all of these are expressions of an increasingly active and modern citizenry. Movements have grown out of each other. The women's movement in Pernambuco, for example (see Chapter 3), grew out of the campaign of rural workers to demand drought relief from the state.

It is the rich world's desire for tropical hardwoods and hamburgers that drives the destruction of the Amazon.

ALLIANCES

But organisation among the poor is not enough. Brazil is a complex and divided society. The social lines of division pass not only between rich and poor, but also within the poor. Many of the sugar mill owners in Triunfo (featured in Chapter 3) are poor men. But they still mercilessly exploit those even poorer than themselves, taking one pound in every ten of the farmers' sugar as the fee for allowing them to mill it. Some Rural Workers' Unions, while fighting for their members' rights, still exclude women from leadership. Conflict still exists between Indian and non-Indian, such as between the gold prospectors and the Yanomami.

Yet no one group of the poor in Brazil holds the key to planning for an alternative, fair and sustainable future. The forging of alliances that can find the common ground is vital, but often difficult. The law governing trade union activity is a major obstacle. Modern industrial unions still do not exist. Instead there is one union per economic sector per geographical area; this fosters craft divisions and narrow local interests. Often it has been easier for women to reach out across sectoral boundaries and find common cause, because they have primary responsibility for everything involved with family care. The women's movement of Paraiba for example links rural women, teachers, domestic servants, and washerwomen.

The story of the building of the Greater Carajás rail line (told in Chapter 7) provides one hopeful example of the poor seeing the problem in broader terms. The CVRD company, which manages the Greater Carajás development area, drove the railway through the land of the Gaviolas Indians. Colonists were located along the tracks. The Indians, however, responded by protesting against the rail line, rather than attacking the colonists. They blocked the tracks, forcing the company to relocate the colonists.

The creation of the Alliance of Forest Peoples in 1989 shows what is possible, when groups sink their differences. Conflict has existed between rubber-tappers and Indians throughout much of this century. There has been violence on both sides. The violence and bitterness of the struggle of the Kaxinawá of Paroá (see Chapters 2 and 5) to free their land from the rubber estates is mirrored elsewhere. But the National Council of Rubber-Tappers and the Union of Indian Nations recognised that they both faced a larger and common problem: the voracious encroachment of big development. In the words of Antonio Macedo of the National Council of Rubber-Tappers: *"If the Indian lands are not safe, we also remain insecure. We used to be enemies with the Indians, but now we form an alliance."*

An alternative and sustainable future for Brazil will have to be created on the basis of an even broader alliance. The emerging demands of the new industrial workers and the long-term need for land reform are all part of the broader picture. It is evident that pressure on the rainforest cannot be relieved without resolving the pressure on land in the north-east and the south, which drives the waves of colonisation. And it is evident that a challenge to the juggernaut of big development is not possible without international action to relieve the massive debt burden on Brazil and open the way for new possibilities. The struggle for

Union meeting of rural workers near Afogados de Ingazeiro, Pernambuco.
(Andrew Couldridge/ Oxfam)

alternatives is not purely national in scope. The Brazilian authorities have argued that what Brazil does with its rainforest, for example, is nobody's concern but their own. But organisations of the poor, who reject this argument, say that the authorities themselves have internationalised the problem through running up the debt and then investing in the Amazon in an attempt to pay it off.

The motive force that drives the destruction of the Amazon is the consumption patterns of the 'developed' world. It is our desire for tropical hardwoods, for Brazilian iron ore, for hamburgers, that determines the pattern of investment. As consumers, we can play a part in changing this; as citizens of the North, we can support solutions to the debt burden. But pardoning the debt will not be enough to save the Amazon, unless the underlying approach to development is changed.

The government of President Collor, which took office in 1990, appears to be more concerned than its predecessors to deal with Brazil's environment problems. The appointment of the ecologist José Lutzenberger as Minister for the Environment was widely seen as a sign of this concern. A smaller proportion of the rainforest was felled and burned in 1990 than in previous years. But there are signs that this respite may be temporary: the new government environmental agency IBAMA is under-resourced, and not able to police the forest; and in October 1990 several 'anti-ecology' candidates won election as state governors. Against the overwhelming vested interests of the big farmers and companies, the test of the government's new determination will be seen by many people in the degree to which its new policies incorporate the aspirations of the poor. A viable alternative can be created only with the participation of the Brazilian people themselves, because the poor have the deepest interest in a real alternative. Our concern for the global consequences of Brazil's development programmes can find effective expression only in support for the initiatives of the poor. And so it is no accident that a book which began with a portrayal of the ecological devastation of the dominant model of development in Brazil should finish with a portrayal of the importance of citizens' actions.

Kaxinawá girl in Paroá village, Acre. (Jenny Matthews/ Oxfam)

NOTES

1 Figures quoted in *The Fate of the Forest*, by Susanna Hecht and Alexander Cockburn (London: Verso, 1989).
2 A hectare is the size of a regulation football pitch.
3 Reprinted with permission from *Fight for the Forest*, by Chico Mendes (London: Latin America Bureau, 1989, p.15).
4 Ibid, pp. 66, 70-71.
5 Quoted in *Passage Through El Dorado* (London: Abacus, 1985, p. 122).
6 *The Last Frontier: Fighting Over Land in the Amazon*, by Sue Branford and Oriel Glock (London: Zed Books, 1985, p. 26).
7 Susanna Hecht and Alexander Cockburn, *The Weekend Guardian*, 25-26 November 1989.
8 *Polo Industrial de Maraba, por dentro e por fora*, February 1989.
9 Ibid.
10 Tancredo Neves died before taking office, and was replaced by José Sarney, his Vice-President.

FURTHER READING

Amazonia, Oxfam Information Department. (Free leaflet.)

Sue Branford and Oriel Glock, *The Last Frontier: Fighting Over Land in the Amazon*. London: Zed Books, 1985.

Catherine Caufield, *In The Rainforest*. London: Heinemann, 1985.

Fight for the Forest: Chico Mendes In His Own Words. London: Latin America Bureau, 1989.

Susanna Hecht and Alexander Cockburn, *The Fate of the Forest: Developers, Destroyers and Defenders of the Amazon*. London: Verso, 1989.

Profile Brazil, London: Catholic Institute for International Relations, 1990.

Trade Unions in Brazil: Fighting Back, London: Brazil Network, 1989.

David Treece, *Bound in Misery and in Iron: The Impact of the Grande Carajás Programme on the Indians of Brazil*. London: Survival International, 1989.

APPENDIX I: MANIFESTO OF THE ALLIANCE OF FOREST PEOPLES

POLICIES FOR DEVELOPMENT FOR FOREST PEOPLES

1 Models of development that respect the way of life, cultures and traditions of forest peoples without destroying nature, and that improve the quality of life.
2 The right to participate in the process of public discussion of all the government projects for forests inhabited by Indians and rubber-tappers, as well as other extractive populations, through the associations and entities that represent these workers.
3 Public guarantees to scrutinise and curb the disastrous impacts of projects already destined for Amazonia, and the immediate halt of projects that damage the environment and Amazonian peoples.
4 Information on policies and projects for Amazonia and any large projects to be subject to discussion in Congress, with the participation of the organisations that represent those people affected by these projects.

AGRARIAN REFORM AND ENVIRONMENT

1 The immediate implementation of extractive reserves in Amazonia in areas indicated by extractive workers and their associations.
2 The immediate demarcation of indigenous lands, placing them under direct control of native populations.
3 Immediate recognition by summary process of all the *colocações* [small communities] of rubber-tappers, giving them immediate land rights.
4 Immediate expropriation of forest areas which are occupied by extractive workers, or of extractive potential.
5 Resettlement in national territory of those of our population thrust into foreign lands by *latifundias* [large agricultural estates].
6 The end to the payment of rent and to the social relations that enslave *seringueiros* [rubber-tappers] on the traditional *seringais* [rubber estate].
7 A policy of zoning that identifies areas inhabited by extractors from areas appropriate for colonisation, and a policy of recuperation of degraded areas.
8 A revision of the policy that seeks to transform indigenous areas into indigenous colonies as proposed by the Calha Norte project.